Argonne Days
in World War I

HORACE L. BAKER

Argonne Days in World War I

Edited with an Introduction by
Robert H. Ferrell

UNIVERSITY OF MISSOURI PRESS
COLUMBIA AND LONDON

Copyright © 2007 by
The Curators of the University of Missouri
University of Missouri Press, Columbia, Missouri 65201
Printed and bound in the United States of America
All rights reserved
5 4 3 2 1   11 10 09 08 07

Library of Congress Cataloging-in-Publication Data
Baker, Horace L. (Horace Leonard), 1893–1948.
    Argonne days in World War I / Horace L. Baker ; edited with an introduction by
Robert H. Ferrell.
        p.   cm.
    Rev. of the 1927 ed. published by Aberdeen Weekly.
    Summary: "A straightforward World War I memoir by Horace Baker, a Mississippi
schoolteacher who took ship for France in the spring of 1918 as a private in the
American Expeditionary Forces and soon fought with the Thirty-second Division in
General Pershing's offensive at the battle of Meuse-Argonne"—Provided by publisher.
    Includes bibliographical references and index.
    ISBN-13: 978-0-8262-1708-0 (hbk. : alk. paper)
    ISBN-10: 0-8262-1708-7 (hbk. : alk. paper)
    1.   Baker, Horace L. (Horace Leonard), 1893–1948.   2.   Argonne, Battle of the,
France, 1918.   3.   World War, 1914–1918—Regimental histories—United States.
4.   United States. Army. Infantry Regiment, 128th—History.   5.   World War,
1914–1918—Personal narratives, American.   I.   Ferrell, Robert H.   II.   Title.
    D545.A63b35   2007
    940.4'36—dc22
                                                                                            2006033106

♾ This paper meets the requirements of the
American National Standard for Permanence of Paper
for Printed Library Materials, Z39.48, 1984.

Designer: *foleydesign*
Typesetter: Bookcomp Inc.
Printer and binder: The Maple-Vail Book Manufacturing Group
Typeface: Goudy

Frontispiece: Horace L. Baker. Courtesy LaVerne Prince.
Title page image: Juvigny, August 1918, preparation for the Meuse-Argonne.

Contents

Acknowledgments

This book owes a great deal to the people who helped. To LaVerne Prince and Hugh Baker, daughter and son of the author. To the Evans Memorial Library of Aberdeen and Mona Gardner of the *Aberdeen Examiner*. To James J. Cooke and John S. D. Eisenhower, readers for the University of Missouri Press. To Stephen Vaughn of the University of Wisconsin, who secured photographs from the William G. Haan papers. To Mitchell A. Yockelson and Timothy K. Nenninger of the National Archives, and Richard J. Sommers, David A Keough, and Richard Baker of the U.S. Army Military History Institute, Army War College, Carlisle Barracks, Pennsylvania. To John Barry, the historian of the Thirty-second Division. To John M. Hollingsworth, the cartographer, and Betty Bradbury, the word processor. To the director of the University of Missouri Press, who makes all books easier, and to her extraordinary managing editor Jane Lago. And to Carolyn, Lorin, and Amanda, the latter a newly added local helper.

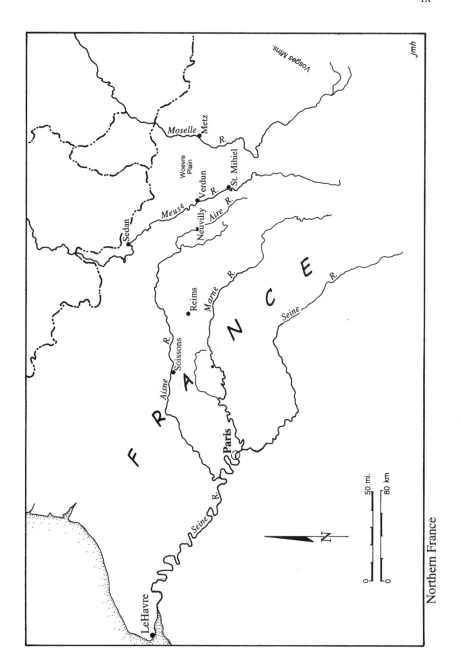

Northern France

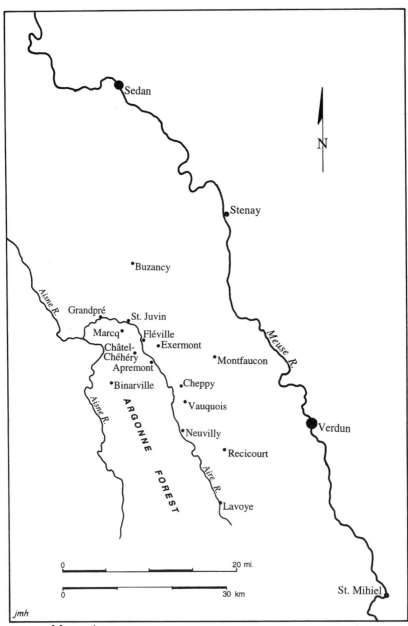

N

Sedan

Stenay

Buzancy

Aisne R.

Grandpré

St. Juvin

Marcq

Fléville

Châtel-
Chéhéry

Exermont

Apremont

Montfaucon

Binarville

Cheppy

ARGONNE

Vauquois

Aisne R.

Neuvilly

Recicourt

FOREST

Aire R.

Meuse R.

Verdun

Lavoye

0   20 mi.

0   30 km

St. Mihiel

jmh

Meuse-Argonne

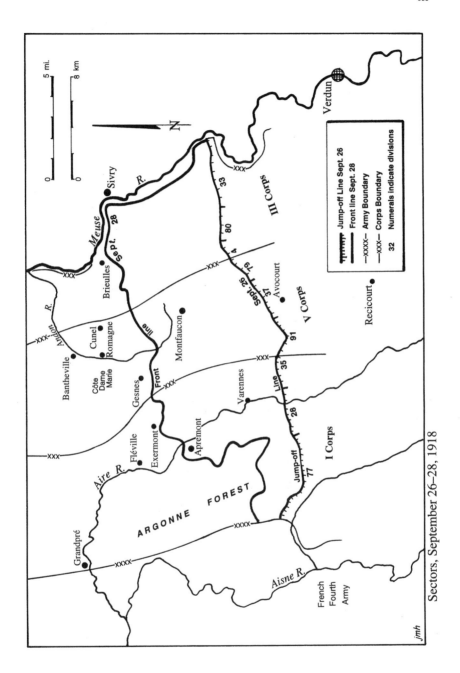

Sectors, September 26–28, 1918

jmh

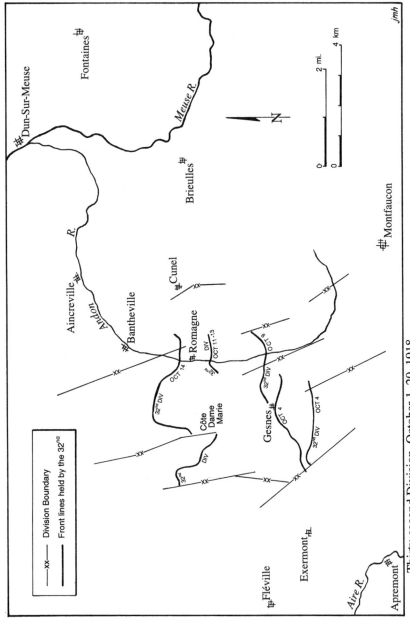

Thirty-second Division, October 1–20, 1918

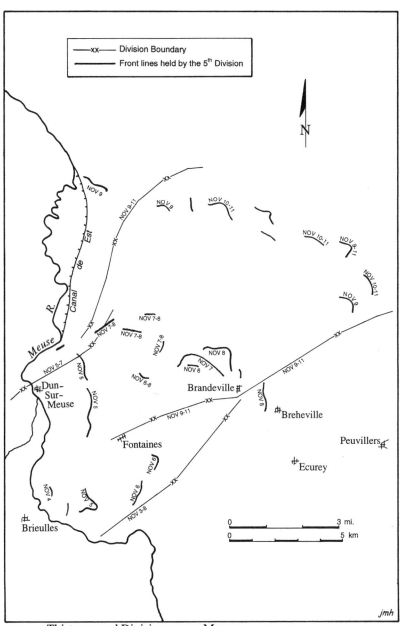

Thirty-second Division across Meuse

Argonne Days
in World War I

Introduction

Argonne Days, by Horace Leonard Baker, is a masterpiece in the literature of American participation in World War I. Baker gives us the war as it was, conveying vividly what it meant to fight for one's country in 1917–1918 in the rear ranks, as the description had it. It is the story of a private, not an officer. One time Baker met Colonel Frank R. McCoy, his regimental colonel in the Thirty-second Division, when McCoy was attempting to get Baker's squad to move more rapidly and pushed him. For the rest of it Baker saw only his fellow soldiers.

Horace Baker took part in a great deal of action. He went overseas to France with the Thirty-ninth Division, which was broken up for replacements, and found himself in Company M, 128th Infantry, in the Thirty-second Division, one of the fightingest divisions in the entire American Expeditionary Forces, the AEF. Made up of National Guard troops from Michigan and Wisconsin, the Thirty-second had been through the Aisne-Marne offensive, in which after the battle of Soissons (which opened July 18, 1918) it helped move the German line back from the Marne River to the Aisne. Before Baker realized what was happening, the division was in the deadliest battle the AEF fought in the war, the great battle of the Meuse-Argonne, which opened on September 26 and ran, in four attacks, one after another, until the armistice of November 11. The battle engaged 1.2 million Americans, the most of any engagement by the U.S. Army in its years of fighting, and was by far the most deadly, with 26,277 men killed and 95,786 wounded. Baker proudly related that he was in the Meuse-Argonne from beginning to end. This was not quite true, for his division was in reserve during the initial attack ending September 29–30. But he was in the second attack

1

and without letup continued into the third, when losses were so heavy that the division commander, Major General William G. Haan, wrote the commander of Fifth Corps, Major General Charles P. Summerall, asking for relief. With gratitude to this fine division and its first-rate commander, the corps commander released the Thirty-second, and it rested until it joined the fourth attack of the battle, beginning November 1 and continuing until the armistice.

This is not the place to set out details about the organization and training of the nearly four million men who entered the U.S. Army in 1917–1918, nor of the army's initial failures in fighting on the battlefields of France against the divisions of Imperial Germany. Suffice to say that on April 6, 1917, when America intervened in the European war that had opened in August 1914, that war turned into a World War. Congress instituted a draft the next month, in May. The cantonments for drafted men and for the men of the National Guard who could be called without national legislation were not ready until September 1917, and many were not finished until the winter of 1917–1918. The initial contingents of drafted men and guardsmen entered federal service in the autumn. Meanwhile the First Division went to France, followed by two more, the Twenty-sixth and Forty-second. The Second Division was organized in France. No more divisions followed until early in 1918, when the first men from the cantonment camps—tent camps in the South, barrack camps in the North—took ship for British and French ports.

The reader of this new edition of *Argonne Days* will ask why American participation in the war had gone on for a year before individuals such as Horace Baker arrived. This was mostly because the administration of President Woodrow Wilson took six months and more to ready the cantonments and also failed to organize the nation's industrial resources to produce ships to take an army to France. In April 1917, the American merchant marine amounted to one million tons, the same tonnage it possessed in the year 1810.

It is true that the Allies did not ask for a massive American army until the end of 1917. There was talk of such an army by Marshal Joseph Joffre, who came over to the United States with a French mission. But the Allies believed that a few divisions would suffice to show the flag. They did not realize what their commanders in France were doing in 1917, which was decimating the ranks of their troops. The French Army attacked early in 1917 in an offensive that took the name of its commander, General Robert Nivelle. The attack was without preparation and cost one hundred thousand casualties, dead and wounded. The British Army attacked in a series of offensives that lasted through the year and took the name of a Belgian town, Passchendaele; troops found themselves fighting in waterlogged fields and trenches, advancing a few kilometers, losing four hundred thousand men in the effort. It was these losses rather than the opportunity that opened for the German Army when Russia withdrew from the war, bringing peace to the eastern front, that made possible a huge German offensive beginning March 21, 1918, and required Allied reinforcement with an American army. Suddenly understanding their predicament, the governments and commanders of France and Britain asked, at the end of 1917, for reinforcements, and the British government offered to withdraw ships from Mediterranean and other runs and bring them over. With a new and highly efficient army chief of staff in Washington, General Peyton C. March, who came into the war department early in March 1918 and turned that department upside down, the army gathered the men and sent them over, among them Horace Baker.

Readers will ask why the U.S. Army, once it reached France in the summer of 1918, suffered such heavy casualties in the Meuse-Argonne. The reason was, in part, the Wilson administration's failure to organize industry, to produce the weapons and munitions to equip the army—planes, artillery, tanks, powder—managing only machine guns and rifles (the Browning machine guns arrived in the war's last weeks). The Allies, mostly the French, furnished weapons and powder, but there were not enough planes, artillery pieces, and tanks. The war department under Secretary Newton D. Baker, a former mayor of Cleveland, was equally inefficient in training the men in the cantonments, allowing training in trench warfare, failing to realize that the German Army was going over to warfare involving elastic attacks and defenses with artillery and machine guns and gas. When the men arrived in France they were virtually without training in a war of movement. They learned by experience, the worst way to learn anything, paying for their instruction with casualties.

Some explanation is necessary about the organization of the American divisions, which was a special problem in the Meuse-Argonne because they were too large and thus awkward to control. The divisions went over in the formation that the commander of the AEF, General John J. Pershing, and a war department commission arranged at the outset of organizing the army in France. Each division consisted of twenty-eight thousand men and officers, which included two infantry brigades of eight thousand men each. Each brigade in turn contained two regiments each of four thousand men. The regiments contained three battalions each of one thousand, with a company size of two hundred and fifty men. In addition, a division contained a brigade of artillery totaling four thousand men, with three regiments of twelve hundred each. Divisions had engineer regiments of twelve hundred, together with other organizations, including machine-gun battalions, ammunition trains, and sanitary (hospital) troops. The Allied and German divisions were half the size of the American divisions, and years after World War I, in the late 1930s, the U.S. Army reduced its divisions to the Allied and German size.

The unwieldy American divisions of 1917–1918, encountering battle first at Soissons, then at St. Mihiel (September 12–16, 1918), and finally in the battle of the Meuse-Argonne, equipped in fair part (but not enough) with French planes, artillery, and tanks, ill trained (prepared for trench warfare when the Germans turned the battlefield into a war of maneuver), stumbled badly in the initial attacks in the Meuse-Argonne. Gradually their performance improved, until in the Meuse-Argonne's last attack beginning November 1 they went forward in triumph, breaking the German main line. Together with the simultaneous attacks of the British and French armies, by this time equally skilled—their near defeat had come the year before—they triumphed against the tired and in its last days disintegrating German Army and won the war.

Not much is known of Horace Baker other than what appears in a slight obituary published years after his death. Before and after his army service he was a teacher and superintendent of schools in Monroe County, Mississippi. He was born in 1893 in Greenwood Springs, Monroe County, Mississippi, a tiny locality in the northeastern portion of the state, close to Alabama. His forebears came from the Carolinas, Tennessee, and Alabama, and one from faraway Indiana. The family took pride in two relatives who became governors of Mississippi, one of whom was the first to live in the governor's mansion.

Horace Baker graduated from high school, a considerable achievement in those bygone years, in 1913. He began teaching that year at his first school, in Quincy Chapel—he had boarded in Amory while attending high school. After his time in the army he taught at Soule's Chapel, the nearby high school. In 1921 he headed the new high school at Greenwood Springs, the first complete high school in the eastern hills of Monroe County. There he taught four years. He attended college at Mississippi Southern, Mississippi State, and the University of Mississippi.

The former army private ran for the superintendency of his county in an election in 1931 and won, taking office for four years beginning the next year. This meant removing to the county seat, Aberdeen, a small and pleasant town of several thousand inhabitants, where he had an office in the courthouse. In 1935, in an election marked by misvoting, miscounting, and one box of ballots being thrown in the river, he was defeated. In 1939 he ran again, successfully. He ran despite an accusation that he was "old patched britches," referring to his dress during the depression years when life was hard. The epithet may have helped, as it made him appear as the simple-living, virtuous person he was. His campaign slogan also helped; recalling for voters the custom of switching mules at a sorghum mill, he urged them to "Hitch me up again." In 1943 he was reelected without opposition. He was defeated in the election of 1947, but the voters of Aberdeen were so pleased with his work as county superintendent that the same year they elected him mayor of the town. He died of a heart attack early in 1948, before he could take office.

Little has survived about his educational theories and ability as a teacher, except that he was an ardent believer in doing one's best with what one has. He came to manhood at the end of the Victorian era and was impressed by the self-help literature of that time, which stressed the importance of striving. He admired students who sought what was good in the world, as in the story "The Blue Flower," by Henry Van Dyke. He told them, "Each of you can find the Blue Flower." A classicist as well as perhaps a sentimentalist, he believed that careful speech was a sign of thought. Everyone, he believed, could learn to speak correctly. When he first became superintendent he proceeded from school to school, visiting each of the 130 schools in the system, and told the students that proper speaking was their heritage, one they must not reject.

The genesis of his book about the Meuse-Argonne was a line-a-day diary he placed in a copy of the Book of Proverbs that had been given to him by the YMCA, making so brief an account of what he saw that it would have no meaning to the Germans if he was captured. He enlarged and expanded upon his notes during the winter of 1918–1919 when billeted in Raubach, Germany. He worked on the account in subsequent years, and in 1927 the *Aberdeen Weekly* published it in book form. It probably was not printed in many copies. A few have survived, including one at the University of Michigan in Ann Arbor, apparently given to the library by an admiring member of the Thirty-second Division.

A note on the editing: everything stands as Horace Baker wrote it, save for minor changes of punctuation and a few factual corrections.

R. H. F.
Ann Arbor
September 1, 2006

1

Chatonrupt

About noon the train stopped at Chevillon, a station on the Marne River, in the Department of Haute-Marne. Chevillon is in a wild, rugged, but entirely beautiful country. The valley of the Marne is here scarcely two hundred yards wide. On the east is a small but long mountain rising almost perpendicularly from the railroad. It is covered with a growth of shrubbery to its summit. On the west the valley wall is lower, but it is still some hill. The village itself clusters around the depot and comprises less than a half-dozen houses. Scant fields are nearby but surely not enough land to support the population.

Disembarking, we lined up. The three fellows I knew best and I managed to get together, a trick we often worked in transfers of this sort. We marched out into a small field near the village, stacked arms, took off our packs, and proceeded to eat the remainder of our corned beef and hardtack. Then we found joy in stretching our cramped limbs. Riding on a Pullman is tiresome even in the U.S.A. Try to imagine, if you never tried it, what forty-two hours on a Cheveaux Limited will do for a fellow. How good the warm sunshine and freedom felt after our long ride in that cold boxcar.[1]

Ah, the memories of that car! It was so crowded that when we lay down to sleep six poor fellows had to stand. They were out-of-luck fellows who neglected to lie down until it was too late. It was piteous to hear them pleading with someone who had a good place on the hard floor to get up and let them sleep an hour only. Turns were sometimes taken but not often.

Our basking in the warm sunshine came soon to a close. Strange officers and corporals appeared among us. Our convoy sergeants with scant adieus hurried away to the train, which soon went back toward St. Dizier and left us to the mercy of the strangers.

7

Soon the sixty-five men of my detachment were marched around and joined to the detachment from B Company. Another wait while one by one the other detachments left the field. When only one other besides ours remained, we too deserted the field and swung into line, marching up the road that hugs the bluff on the west side of the Marne.

Never shall I forget that march! Often in a reminiscent mood I go over the route again, and am prone to believe that it was the pleasantest march of all my army career. As I said the road ran up the west side of the river next to the valley wall. Sometimes we were in sunshine but more often in shadow, for the sun was well past its meridian when we started. When we had left Massay, two hundred miles to the south, a week before, it was still that dreamy and glorious season that in a far happier clime we call Indian summer. Here a touch of winter was already in the air. Leaves were already beginning to fall; the most of them were green yet. That indefinable feeling that betokens autumn was unmistakably present, and the heart cannot but beat in unison with it.

And the march, in keeping with the season, was slow and leisurely as if there never more would be hurry. This was in marked contrast to the Thirty-ninth [Division], which did everything snappily. I must say I liked the change. Judging from our gait we had the afternoon to make the trip. Stops were frequent, and welcome, for though we needed exercise, as hungry as we were and consequently weak, a little exercise soon tired us. Nor could we fail to notice the absence of the angrily barked command that we had been used to in the old outfit.

A melancholy silence brooded over all the landscape, and it was oppressive after the constant roar of the train and jolt of a flat-wheeled car. The ominous stillness was broken at intervals by a burst of rifle fire, which came ever and anon from over the hills to our right. Evidently some small detachment was practicing at a rifle range, but the sounds were warrish sure.

So, leisurely up the road we marched, not knowing whither or to what outfit we were going. Passing through one small village and by another, we drew up ten kilometers from the starting point in the village of Chatonrupt, so pleasantly remembered by so many men.

Chatonrupt is a village of two streets; one is the road up the Marne Valley; the other comes down a tributary valley from the west. The valley here is wider than at Chevillon. The railroad passes beyond the river and through a newer village whose name I never learned. Another railroad is atop the steep western hills. The village is an old, old one, in a wild, eerie place, and a solemn hush was pervading everything. Was it the bated breath of a country near to the seat of war?

Turning up the street to the right, we halted. A bugle call echoed and re-echoed down the valley. It was the retreat call. So we stood retreat in the street of Chatonrupt with full packs at five o'clock, which was an hour earlier than we had been accustomed to in the formation at Massay. Then, while the old men of the outfit stationed there went to supper, we new men were sorted out and assigned to different companies.

In transfers like this, one's thoughts are always on whether or not he will be separated from his friends. Three friends were now with me—Glen W. Evans, whose post office in old Mississippi was (and is) the same as mine. He alone of all the thirty-five brave boys who left Aberdeen with me was still at my side. Fermon Hughes from the day he walked into my tent at [Camp] Beauregard to speak to Evans had been my friend. Then there was Andrew Shirey from Winfield, Alabama, destined not to return from France, whom I had met in a leisure moment on the good ship *Huron* at Brest. Not wishing to be separated, we had got together thinking it the only plan.

An officer walked down the line picking out the largest men. Afraid he would choose me, I drew myself up as much as possible. He was choosing stretcher bearers. I am still glad he missed me. Evans had had some experience as a telephone lineman, but a call for them elicited no response from him. Finally those left of us were moved down on another street. A detail was counted off from each end of the line and marched away. This left only twenty-six of us, the windup of the assorting. We were assigned to "M" Company of the 128th Infantry. Our wisdom in staying together kept us four buddies from separating again. Upon inquiry, we found that our new command was none other than the Fighting Thirty-second, which we were told was a "shock" division. This phrase when explained to us gave us a shock, for it was said its duty was to go where other units failed and break the German line.

Then there was supper down on the bank of the famous River Marne. It consisted of nothing but corned beef and coarse French bread, but there was plenty of it and a warm welcome by the cook, Bill Millard, who kept opening beef tins until we, full for the first time since we came to France, had to go off and leave some uneaten. It was not so bad to be in a shock division if we had plenty to eat.[2]

When billets were assigned, Shirey was separated from the other three of us. We were put into a nice warm barn and had some half-dozen as agreeable companions as I ever met in the army. Our welcome was sincere, the whole bunch was jovial, one boy passed around some apples even, and we decided we were glad of our transfer. A nice warm bed of hay completed the day.[3]

September 21

Reveille was at an early hour and followed by a good breakfast in which pancakes and syrup were the chief attraction and very, very welcome.

I bathed my hands and face that morning in the clear waters of the Marne. Here it was only a creek and was so clear that, though it was two feet deep in midstream, every pebble in the bed could be distinctly seen. I could not help watching its crystal waters swiftly passing and thinking of the two big battles that had been fought on its lower course, and how its limpid waters had been stained red with the blood of soldiers shed in a war that we too in a few days would be fighting in.[4]

Instead of drill, the company, marching up the tributary valley, came to a rifle range a mile or so from town, and that rifle range! I could not help smiling; it was a row of tomato cans on stakes against the opposite hillside. We new fellows shot first and did well. My coach in this was a nice little noncom named Kennedy. It was his fate to lose his life the last week of the war.

After dinner there was rifle inspection. And such an inspection! In contrast to the snappy Thirty-ninth where all inspections were made by commissioned officers, our company commander now took his stand to one side while the sergeants walked up and took our guns as one of the boys said, "Just as if he didn't give a d—n whether he inspected it or not."

Back at the billet after inspection I inquired where the apples we had eaten the night before had come from. I was informed that there was a tree just back of the barn and that the boys were accustomed to help themselves. So I repaired thither and found a fine tree with lots of excellent apples thereon. It was just a little way up the hillside. There were quite a few apples on the ground and I began filling my pockets when, as usual, I noticed those on the tree looked better. So, I began to shake the limbs when suddenly a loud commanding voice at the rear door of the barn sang out, "Hey, there, you, don't you know better than to take the Frenchman's apples? I've been watching for whoever was doing it. Now I've caught you; you needn't run; it's too late."

I won't ask you to imagine the dozen thoughts that ran through my mind in an instant. Part of them were: "Yes, I have stepped right into the trap; the fellows were good to me to get me caught"; "I'll suffer for all the apples that have been stolen"; "Here I am in a new division and a blot on my service record that I have tried to keep so clean"; "It'll be some record to start on in a new outfit"; "It will be the guardhouse sure"; "I'll not let him see that I'm scared but will be brave as possible"; "If I'm going to the guardhouse, likely I'll need some apples." So taking a few more apples, even though I was scared so badly I was in a tremble, I walked off along the hillside. I was the worst scared I ever was in while a soldier and not on the front.

And did the officer come on and arrest me and take me with him? To my surprise he went toward the apple tree. Why did he care how many I had taken? Then, oh boy, I discovered that he was only a private and had a desire for apples too. But I didn't go back to the tree, not I, that day.

At retreat that afternoon the new men were organized into the fourth platoon. Sergeant Fosse, the most soft-spoken noncom I ever saw and one of the nicest, was made platoon sergeant. I was made one of the acting corporals, though all were to lose their jobs three days later.

At this formation I noticed that the company commander was a first lieutenant, a line sergeant was acting as top sergeant, and that there was only one second lieutenant. When I inquired where the captain and other officers were, I received this reply:

"Captain Rowles was killed at Juvigny on the Soissons front, the other officers were wounded; First Sergeant Ryan was hit by eleven machine-gun bullets but was alive at last account." I understand that he recovered but he did not return to the company.

Just here, I want to say that, while I still to some degree share the dislike of officers common to privates, no company ever had a finer commander than First Lieutenant Pelton or a better second lieutenant than McKee. Murphy, the acting top, could be a fine fellow when he chose to be.[5]

All that Saturday afternoon trucks had been arriving and were being parked down on the Marne street. It looked ominous to me and the old men with sage shakes of the head often said, "Boys, that means another trip to the front."

On the whole my opinion of the Thirty-second was favorable. We had been nicely treated by everyone and I had decided that if I could not fight with the Thirty-ninth then I was glad I was a part of the Thirty-second, called by the French "Les Terribles."

And the war came close to me that night. In the dead hours of night, I judge about 2:30 in the morning, I went into the street for a drink of water. The beautiful full moon was looking down on a village as quiet as a city of the dead and silvering over the landscape. I doubt if there was a living soul stirring in the village except myself. I was looking at the moon and the front glistening in the moonlight and shivering from the icy tinge in the air, when suddenly faint and far away, borne on the crisp air of the night, came the sound of big guns at the front. I listened and there were more of them. I cannot describe the thrill or the emotions I experienced as I heard the guns of war for the first time. Yet it was only an incident of a four-year war.

2

Lavoye

September 22

Sunday morning was bright and clear. As all soldiers know it is the army's Monday. This particular Sunday we had orders to stick close to our billets. Most of us stayed in them. About the only time I got away from mine was when I went down the street and across the other to buy a small quantity of delicious white grapes. We whiled away the time with talk and reading what we had at hand, which consisted of little save Testaments and a week-old Paris edition of an American newspaper. I read the latter a time or two and quite a bit in my Testament but still time hung heavily on my hands.[1]

While perusing the casualty list, one of my comrades found his own name in the list of the dead. Poor fellow! He was destined soon to be really among the dead as was also his bunkie, who was one of the best swearers I ever heard. I think he meant little harm by it and his expletives kept us in a continual roar of laughter, whether directed against the conduct of the war or whether at whatnot. Sad it is when I remember the going of those amiable fellows, for three of the nine in that billet were sleeping beneath the sod when Armistice Day came.

Dinner came; after it, we were given our supper in our mess kits, then we rolled packs. About three o'clock we marched down and boarded the waiting trucks. Here I got my first sight of the fighting old warhorse, Colonel McCoy. He got in a hurry to get the line to give way to let some trucks pass, just before we got on the trucks, and in his eagerness put out his hands and tried to push the line back by pushing against the chests of two soldiers, one of whom was yours truly. It was a thrill to be touched by a real live colonel, and that colonel my own, and I realized as never before that I was part, really an integral part, of the army. I always liked Colonel McCoy, and sometimes wonder if that little incident aided my liking.[2]

I had to board a truck that contained only one of my squad, a fellow Mississippian named Culpepper, but then there were only fourteen on the truck while some had twenty-two. Some of the drivers of this convoy were Indo-Chinese, but ours happened to be a Frenchman. Shortly before four, we pulled out, none of us knew whither, but all of us were sure that we were on our way to the front.

There was no noncom on the truck. Bobrelli, originally from sunny Italy and one of the most likable fellows I ever knew from that country, and I were acting corporals. The whole bunch not excepting the Italian corporal treated me with all the deference that they would, had I been put in command of the truck. This was new to me but I tried to live up to the best qualities of the rank, and even today my heart goes out in gratitude to the dandy fellows that were my comrades on that trip for their deference.

The composition of the personnel of the crowd was quite American. There were five men from West Virginia, three from Mississippi, and one each from Virginia, Pennsylvania, Kentucky, Missouri, Arkansas, and Louisiana.

An hour from Chatonrupt we ate supper while the truck was in motion. At a village a little farther on, some of the boys got a bottle of wine and drank it. It was followed by another. I did not drink any but had really given them permission to do so and when some of them began to get a little tipsy I had almost a wish that I had forbidden it. However, I figured that it might be the last time for some of them, as indeed it was for several, and I thought if they wanted to indulge I ought not to object. Not all of them drank, though most did.

Shortly after we started, somebody started up a song. Snatches of all the army songs were sung, I think, and the more the wine took effect the better was the singing. Ever the song most reverted to was "Are You from Dixie?" Morgan, the Pennsylvanian, assisted by Bobrelli were the leaders in the singing, Morgan singing the song named with great fervor. Brave soldier! He was destined never to see the front line, let alone Dixie or Pennsylvania again.

Just before dark we passed through St. Dizier. All afternoon it had been clouding up and soon after dark it began to rain—one of those characteristic French rains. Unable to see the landscape longer, we tried to get what sleep we could, and so through the rain and the mud and the blackness we went jogging onward.[3]

Of course, none of us knew to what sector we were headed, but we were sure that there was to be a great American drive and knew that there was need for the Thirty-second to be there.

September 23

I slept fairly well, part of the time on the hard bench and part on the packs on the floor of the truck. Once I was awakened by startled French cries as the truck went backward. It scared me badly but no harm was done.

About four o'clock the truck stopped and an American voice outside inquired who we were. When told, he said, "You may as well get off here." Another voice said, "Better let them go on to ——." I did not catch the name of the place but, when we asked how far it was, was told "four miles." Sometime later we were again stopped and a commanding voice gave us to know that we were to unload.

I raised the curtain and looked out. Never in all my experience have I looked upon a drearier scene. It was raining and had been all night. The road was a river of mud and there was not a house or light in sight. Only one or two other camions disgorging their load of soldiers relieved the monotony of the rain-soaked fields and equally rain-soaked woods in the distance.[4] Yet in the face of all of this I was conscious of a fierce, wild joy, strange as it may seem.

Clambering down from the truck after most of the boys had got off, I heard one of them say, "There he is," and a man in an officer's coat walked up to me. It was our major.

He directed that I take my men down the road to where I would find the rest of the company. We started that way. And now will the reader try to imagine my predicament? The company didn't seem easy to find, and here I was in command of thirteen Yanks on a forsaken road, in the mud and rain and darkness and not knowing where we were supposed to go, in other words lost "somewhere in France."

Two hundred yards or so down that dreary road, we espied a group of men emerging from a dark field on the left of the road in single file. Glory be. It was M Company, or a part of it, and my detachment fell in line behind them; maybe they knew where they were going, at least my responsibility was over.

At a fork of the road we took the left. During our three-mile hike up that road daylight slowly came and the rain gradually ceased. On our way we gathered up many small groups of our men and when we stopped and fell out to rest had nearly the whole company.

The usual rest spell was fifteen minutes, but this dragged into an hour and finally into three and we Yanks were still there beside the road and wanting to go to some other place no matter where. Fitful gusts of rain came and the raw wind chilled us to the bone. In addition to being wet and cold, there was a gnawing of the stomach, for there was no semblance of breakfast and worst of all some soldiers were lost. I am sure from the expression of their faces that the officers were as much at sea as we.

At length a lone French soldier came by. From him we learned we were on the Verdun front and that the line was some twenty-five miles away. We thought it strange that no guns were firing, though I learned later that even warriors abate their work when it rains to some extent. But the theater of war was surely near, for I have a vivid recollection of twice passing through woods filled with huge piles of shells of all sizes and buzzing trucks on our rounds somewhere that morning.

Near noon, we backtracked for two miles and pitched camp a half kilometer east of the road down in a little valley. I won't mention some iron rations eaten for it was forbidden to eat them but will say thirst soon drove me to take the squad's canteens and others' and set out in quest of water.[5] I did not mean to go so far but fell in with a number of others with similar object, and when I found water it was at the public fountain in the village of Lavoye two kilometers from camp.

Proof that I was one of the luckiest men in the army can be found here, for I had just returned to camp when orders came to roll packs and march away. Imagine what a pickle I would have been in had the company gone while I was away.

Lavoye is not unpleasantly remembered, nor is the crossroads nearby where a cool and efficient military police was directing a traffic of beaucoup trucks and transport of all kinds. Something told me this spot was a target for German guns.[6]

As I said it was moving day again. We came back to the road and, after traveling back the way we had come for about two kilometers, turned into a dim road that branched off to the right. Soon this became a path plain and well traveled but without apparent reason faded into a dim trail that eventually merged with the woodland and left us traveling through the underbrush that was still wet from the morning's rain. About a kilometer of such and we came out into a large clearing or rather under a grove, for the underbrush had been cut and piled, leaving the large trees standing. This clearing embraced a narrow valley and the surrounding hillsides, and I judge there were some thirty acres cleared. A weathered and it seemed unused house, built of wood, was at the head of the valley, rather on the slope above it, and another on the crest of the ridge to the left. It was not altogether an uninviting place and I felt we had reached our camping ground.

On the far hillside we pitched camp. We were now about five miles from the place where we left the trucks and the day was far spent. Shortly the rolling kitchens came in, and although we had had no breakfast or dinner, there was a substantial and welcome supper. About dark, orders came to me to caution my squad not to smoke outside their tents, for fear of being seen by enemy air scouts.

September 24

The first thing on Tuesday morning (September 24), we acting corporals were to lose our jobs. The company was reorganized and the new men mixed up with the old, a splendid idea. I became number one in the front rank of the second squad of the third platoon. I was glad of the change for I had been wondering how I would lead a squad over the top; now the responsibility was gone.

My new corporal was Amos Steen of Patten, Maine. I have never been worse mistaken in my first estimate of a fellow, for I felt sure I would not like him, but soon got to liking him quite well. Although he was then only a lad of nineteen, as they told me, he was a husky giant almost, and already grim-visaged by war. A few days after this he put on his second service stripe that betokened that he had been overseas one year. No one was more intimately connected with my battle experiences than Corporal Steen.

After reorganizing, we drilled. It was mostly open-order drill. We new fellows had had little of that, and those old men knew that that was all that was used on the front. Steen had disappeared for some reason and a private named Konkle who was later to become our corporal when Steen was made sergeant drilled us. He was a good fellow and knew the drill thoroughly.[7]

About nine o'clock from the frail wooden building atop the hill came a sweet insinuating sound. Immediately the command, "Get under cover, hostile airplane." Clustered close together under a tree like chickens when a hawk is near, we stood motionless for a time while from far to the northeast came the sound of explosions; "Anti-aircraft guns" the old men said. I wondered how they could tell. When I became an "old" man myself, I knew only too well and the sounds were only too familiar, but I cannot tell the reader how they sounded and if he doesn't already know I hope he will never find out.

Back to our drill, but soon the sound came again and we like the barnyard fowls scampered to cover again. This time airplanes flew over us, but I cannot say that they were Boche machines.

In the afternoon we camouflaged our pup tents by cutting bushes and putting over them. This was part of the great plan by which all troop movements before the last drive were hidden from the enemy.[8]

Wednesday, September 25

I awoke sometime before reveille with the sounds of a distant but terrific barrage ringing in my ears. Actually, now the war was close at hand, I was even hearing a tremendous barrage. After reveille the "old" men said, "Somebody's going over the top this morning. Hope it's some outfit as good as the Thirty-second."

With the guns still booming, we went out to drill. Maybe the military sounds didn't put pep into us, but I think they did. War was coming close to home to us and we might be in battle any day now. Indeed, I had a curious warhorse feeling that I wanted to get into the fray. But the booming died away and drilling became the same humdrum affair it had ever been.[9]

It was a hard day's drilling, but the last for many days, and quite a few boys had finished their drilling forever. Just before dark we rolled packs, policed up, and sat down to wait. I experienced a peculiar homeless feeling I had not felt when the tents were standing. At twilight we lined up, right-faced, and marched away. Perhaps not one of us has ever returned to those woods.

3

A Long Night March

Of all the marches I ever made, that of the night of September 25 will be the last to fade from my memory. I can never accurately describe it. How one's emotions varied! One moment he was on fire with hope and fervor and patriotism; the next sunk in the depths of despair. One moment dog-tired, the next as full of pep as ever.

We marched over the hill and through the dark woods in columns of twos. No one knew where we were bound, but most of us had a good idea. I had little desire to talk to my buddies so listened to Otto McKinley, giant from the hills of West Virginia, ask some dozens of questions of his big corporal, Ogden, from Wisconsin, who marched just in front of me. His painstaking answers to those questions constituted my first lesson on the composition of an army, how many squads, platoons, companies, battalions, regiments, brigades, divisions, corps, armies, etc., it took to make the next higher designation.

Often as I stumbled along through the darkness I almost lost my way, but ever and anon I could see the huge bulk of the burly corporal looming in the darkness. Across a hollow or two and we came out into a muddy road. How I did dread a march over a road of slush. But the mud soon gave place to a firm rock road.

We came to a crossroads and turned to the left. We entered a deserted village and at the far side stopped to rest. For some reason the place looked familiar. I looked closely and recognized Lavoye, although I had thought our route led in the opposite direction. I feel sure no other enlisted man in the battalion knew its name. We were now two miles on our way.

The rest period was prolonged. It began to rain softly as though the heavens were weeping over the sacrifice of so many lives that was so soon to be made. Yanks always want to go someplace else, so becoming impatient the cry "Let's go" resounded through the streets that were deserted save for us soldiers.

Two incidents of that first two miles did much to lower my morale. The first was a remark of a YMCA man as he stood aside to let us pass: "Let the boys going to the trenches pass." Then in a changed tone he added, "What a pity for such a fine bunch of men to go into battle." It would have been better to have been unsaid. From him we learned we were near Verdun, though I think that the term "near" was a relative one. The other incident was worse, and happened shortly afterward. A truck bound to the rear was piled high with something. After it passed two or three of the fellows declared that it was loaded with the bodies of dead soldiers, averring that they could distinguish their feet. I know now that it wasn't so, but was prepared to believe anything, and so as far as the hearers of the remarks were concerned it might as well have been.

And a memory persists of somewhere on that hike seeing a light at a crossroads and a voice in haste calling, "Let the gas man by: they need it at the front," and a whirring motorcycle as an accompaniment. I felt like one in a dream when it happened, for everything was so unreal. So it seems a memory of a dream.[1]

About the time the march was resumed the rain ceased. Up a small hill at the edge of the town and we came out upon a broad tableland. Such a sight! It seemed we were facing southeast, but I know it must have been northeast. In a wide semicircle from the left to the right, there was a lurid hue. A livid flash like lightning cleft the night afar off, which changed in a moment to inky blackness to be succeeded in a moment by two or three other flashes of varying intensity and at various places on the horizon. A brilliance here, darkness there, flash followed after flash, and from afar came a dull report like distant thunder. Awestricken by the sight, we new men stumbled forward silently, never looking once at the road but gazing always at the fireworks.

Looking at the verisimilitude of an impending storm, and truly one was coming but not of rain and thunder and lightning, but of shells and bullets and sudden death, I could not help but wonder how far off the trenches were, if they were up-to-date or only rude ditches, if we would have casualties before we got there, how long we would stay in the trenches before the big drive began, and if I would get through it. It seemed somewhat unlikely that I would but I never once lost hope entirely.[2]

There was still the possibility that we would not go into the ditches that night, but most of us had decided we would. The last vestige of hope that we were not going into battle vanished when Ogden sang out, "Steen, you can see where we are headed for now; back to the front for us."

Steen replied, "Sure we are."

But war was what had brought us across three thousand miles of ocean, and if battle were to be our part, why, we'd be soldiers still, and while like myself many of the boys experienced a sinking in the region of the heart no doubt, still no word of fear was spoken.

Even in the most serious moments there is always some levity. The boys laughed and joked each other. When the step was faster than common or the time when a rest should have been taken was allowed to pass unnoticed and the hike continued, someone always had something to say about running the colonel's horse down or wondering if he only had one flat tire if he happened to be in his car. And all the while fatigue and utter weariness were gaining ground and sleep beckoned us the more.

But there was no time for sleeping, though once when we passed through a well-nigh destroyed village silvered over with moonlight, for the moon had at last broken through the clouds, the temptation to fall out and rest beneath its inviting walls was intense. But there was no halt and the ruins of the tenantless village echoed and reechoed the tramp of an armed host bent on avenging its destruction and sped it on into the open country and straight toward the circle of fire.

More livid the fireworks became; now and then a rocket could be seen; the dull thunder grew louder and war as a whole more ominous. Many and varied were the emotions now. One moment the heart was filled with the fiercest military fervor—the kind that makes victory possible; the next it was possessed of the tenderest thoughts of home, without which victories do not occur. Now one was glad he was there; in a moment he wished he was thousands of miles away. And when close beside the road we saw a soldier's grave, evidently French, all war's grim reality came home to us with a thud.

The front was in a state of excitement that night, it was easy to guess that. Rockets and flares went up by the scores, cannon boomed right and left of us, motorcycles and automobiles sped by us. Once when French helmets were plainly distinguishable in a car, someone muttered, "French war gods." Each and every one of us felt instinctively that something was soon to happen, that an American drive, the greatest up to this time, was at hand. The only things that had been told us were vague surmises by the noncoms who likely knew for certain little more than the privates. It is surprising, however, to think back on the time just previous to the Meuse-Argonne and realize how well even the most ignorant private was posted as to what was about to happen. Many talked of peace in a matter-of-fact way as if they were sure it would come at the end of the drive, and it happened as we privates planned, not because of our planning but in some measure at least because of the way we carried out the leaders' plans.

For hours the march continued. It seemed that we would neither stop nor reach the trenches, but they were getting appreciably nearer.

Suddenly, about ten o'clock, on our left something happened. Hundreds of guns sent over a fierce barrage. The roar was terrible, awe-inspiring. Had the big show begun? Would we just march into battle without taking to the trenches at all? No, the barrage was not the beginning to the show, but it was the prelude. For an hour it lasted, then settled into a sullen angry roar.[3]

Onward the 128th marched straight toward the lines. On the outskirts of the village of Jubecourt we descried a rest camp, that is, a cemetery; there is no other rest camp for a soldier. We almost envied the dead, for they were at peace, but we knew neither rest nor peace. The graves had been freshly dug—perhaps some contained American soldiers—more of war's grim horrors pressed home.

Jubecourt was a deserted village and a well-nigh destroyed one. It was silent as the tomb and the echo of our hobnails on its rock streets was uncanny. In the heart of the town near the church we halted, many of the men lying down in the street where they stood when we halted and going to sleep in a few moments, but I was too tired to sleep. Presently Lieutenant Pelton, the company commander, came along. Because the men had not got out of the street to lie down he grumbled a bit, the only time I ever heard him do so, but he was right about it for a truck could not have passed until the street was cleared, which would have taken some time.

From Jubecourt the road led down a precipitous hill. The moon far to the west cast weird, uncanny shadows on the eastern side of the town. While the part of the town on the top of the hill was bathed in moonlight, that clinging to the eastern slope and in the valley below was lost in deepest shadow except where straggling moonbeams found their way through the ruins. Somehow a queer feeling came over me. It seemed that this was all a dream and I would awake and find it so, or that I was in the realms of enchantment.

There was some commotion at the foot of the hill and an outcry or two. Some soldiers not in line were there, but I have never found out the cause of the excitement. A long hill beyond called forth strength to climb, and I realized that I was not dreaming and was very much in the land of the living ere I reached the top and got a new and closer view of the fireworks in the battle line.

Midnight passed and we marched on. The boys were holding on well, and if any of my company mates fell out I did not know it. Finally we went through the ruined village of Recicourt and surmounted the hill beyond. Just as I had decided that we would walk right into the trenches, we halted.

We were near the trenches now, it was certain, for it seemed that the flares were rising from just over the hill, but the trenches were not to be our portion that night. My platoon went far down on the steep hillside, and Shirey and I, unrolling our blankets, made our bed there in the long grass on which the frost glittered like diamonds in the now feeble moonlight. The crisp autumn air made blankets comfortable, and we were soon blissfully lost to the terrors of war. What a blessing sleep is.

4

The First Day of the Meuse-Argonne

I am sure that I had not been asleep but an hour or so when I awoke with a start. Yes, I was terrified too. Of all the sounds ever heard, the most awful was now rending the air. Hell had broken loose; no other term even approaches a description. The great drive we were all anticipating had begun; the preliminary barrage was going over.[1]

Of all barrages, surely it was the worst. From far west to distant east the elements were aglow. Flares still came up over the hill and as far away on either hand as the eye could see, and they had been multiplied manifold. And above all was the din, the mighty roar of the heavy artillery, the shriek of shells as they sped on their mission of destruction, and the sharper crack of the lighter guns. There was no intermission and no variation; there was no distinguishing one gun from its fellows but all mingled in a fearful din. The screeching of shells blended into a mighty wail. The booming of the guns gave a crackling sensation like as if the sounds accompanying the burn-ing of a house were magnified a thousand times. The word "hell" gives but a faint idea of what I am trying and failing to describe.

Then there was the consciousness that amid all the crackling inferno I was listening to were thousands of American boys like me, to whom life was just as sweet, country was as dear, and death as fearful, and that some of them were dying. For the life of me I could not imagine how any could escape that awful place. And then there was the realization that in a short time I too would be where blood ran freest. Perhaps, even, I would be there before morning, for the din seemed to take its beginning just over the hill and we could eas-ily manipulate the distance.

I called softly to my bunkie. He too was awake and listening. Poor fellow. He was never destined to emerge from the Meuse-Argonne.

Valiant American. He fell that day some weeks later when we took Romagne. The sods of France never covered a truer friend, a braver patriot, or a better Christian than he. He had heard the first guns of the drive but was fated not to hear the last.

Neither of us being in a mood of conversation, little was said. I fell to musing over the hell that mortals will create here on earth for each other, but sheer weariness soon overtook me, and although the din rolled on sleep lost me its horrors.

It was daylight when again I awoke. The morning air was chilly. The barrage continued but the cannonading was much subdued. Overhead an Allied airplane slowly took its way to the rear. The sun was still below the horizon. It was the time when the front fellows were going over the top. My regiment had made no move toward getting up, and doubtless most of the fellows were still asleep. Save for the uneven places covered by o.d. blankets, no one would have guessed that a whole regiment was bivouacked on that hill.[2] Our part in the first day of the great drive was now clear to me. We were in reserve. I had feared that we would go in, relieve some division, and make the attack ourselves.

Soon the sun thrust itself above the horizon and shone full upon me. Despite the fleecy clouds that flocked the sky the sun was looking down in splendor on the world's greatest battlefield and on the greatest drama ever yet enacted by Americans. By a queer turn of fate the descendants of those pioneers of the new land called America had now come back to the lands that their fathers had left in search of liberty and a new chance in life, to stabilize that same old world.[3]

I sat up and looked around. Above me rose a huge sloping hill; across a narrow valley, a similar hill appeared; to the left could be seen the housetops of Recicourt. A few planes flew here and there within our range of vision and an observation balloon or two arose on the right. Down in the valley was a narrow-gauge railway, and up it came a train loaded with blue-coated French soldiers, evidently some of the ones relieved the night before by the last of the Americans to enter the lines. As there was no reveille and no chow call, I tried to sleep some more but failed, and when the other boys got up I did likewise.

A short while afterward, the news spread through the regiment that "The front-line boys went over the top at 5:30 and drove everything before them. The Germans broke and fled and the Yanks are now pursuing them."

Almost simultaneously, as if to kill our joy at this good news, there was a loud explosion on the hilltop some two hundred yards from me. It was followed at intervals by others. German shells! I was now under shellfire! Ah, what a quick change. I was under shellfire just three months to a day from the day I left home. Before noon an M Company man was shell-shocked and a K Company sergeant from Colorado had a hunk knocked out of his shin with a fragment of a shell.

As I said, we were in reserve just back of the lines. Months after I learned more of the situation at that time. It might not be a bad idea to say something of the other divisions and their disposition.

This region in the northeast of France had been selected by General Pershing as the theater of American operations. In the eastern part of our sector was the valley of the Meuse River; on the west was the Argonne Forest; in the center was a broad ridge since called by some writers the "whaleback." At the beginning of the battle, two of our divisions, the Twenty-sixth and Twenty-ninth, were east of the Meuse, and they gave a good account of themselves.[4]

The line from the Meuse to the Argonne was about twenty-eight miles in length and was held by nine divisions.

Next to the Meuse was the Third Corps comprising the Thirty-third, Eightieth, and Fourth divisions in line from east to west and the Third Division in corps reserve. West of the Third Corps was the Fifth Corps, which had in line the Seventy-ninth, Thirty-seventh, and Ninety-first divisions with the Thirty-second in corps reserve. Holding the west flank was the First Corps, with the Thirty-fifth, Twenty-eighth, and Seventy-seventh divisions in line and the Fifth in corps reserve. In army reserve were the veteran First, Second, and Forty-second divisions.[5] It will thus be seen that the newer divisions were in the lines at the beginning of the fray, while those that had seen some battle experience were in corps reserve and that the divisions that had seen most service were far back in army reserve. It will also be seen that as we were supporting the middle corps our position was just back of the center of the line and a few miles south of what had been the village of Avocourt.

About ten o'clock word came that all who wished might attend services in the battered little church in the village. I didn't feel inclined to go for I thought that a formal lip service at that time would be only a hollow mockery. I was realizing that religion was an affair of the heart, and I was getting ready for the terrible ordeal I was soon to undergo. Few, if any, went to church.

Then came the order to roll packs and get ready for dinner. So my stay under the apple tree on the hillside was finished. Dinner consisted of a predominance of sweetened tomatoes. I like them without the sweetening but I could not relish them with it, although I had had no breakfast.

Immediately after dinner, we slung packs and leisurely wended our way down the hill and across the valley. Partway up the opposite hillside we halted and deployed in platoon column. In this fashion we moved forward along the hillside toward the battle lines. Quite a magnificent sight that—a regiment in four columns fifty yards apart, the companies being an equal distance from each other. I looked back across the valley and, lo, another regiment advanced there (probably the 127th), covering the hillside like a swarm of grasshoppers.

A kilometer on our way for some reason I got a short distance behind my platoon. They were surrounding a small hillock when I started to run and catch up with them but decided to take a near cut and run up the mound. But I didn't. Imagine my surprise to find just as I reached it that it wasn't a hill at all but was a huge pile of shells for big guns, covered over with the all too familiar (afterward) burlap foliage. Could it have been seen and recognized from an airplane? Well, I hardly reckon so.

Another half mile onward and we were approaching the line of observation balloons, when we had staged for us my first sight of air warfare. Frederick Palmer mentioned this in his book, *Our Greatest Battle*, but he fell far short of describing it, as likely I will.

A German aviator, having daringly crossed the fronts and made an attack on the first observation balloon on our right, sent it to the ground in flames, then despite the anti-aircraft guns that blazed away at him, wheeling around, he brought down the next one. Then he sailed away toward his base, but it was only a ruse for in a few moments he was back again and destroyed two more in the same order. I guess he called it a day then, for he returned no more. I think all the observers escaped safely after a parachute journey. The balloon in our immediate front came down almost to earth hurriedly. So here was sure-enough war right before my eyes.

Our path led down into a deep valley where a French railroad ran along under the lee of the opposite hill. This hill was about as steep as I ever climbed, but we clambered up it after a while. The Germans were shelling the railroad about two hundred yards to our left but couldn't hit it for the hill. While passing through the apple orchard on top of the hill I chanced to see an enemy shell explode in midair. Already I was beginning to feel like a veteran, and could I have been back at home, what tales of the war I could have told!

Two miles farther and we began to pass shallow trenches and new dugouts, one of which, though unfinished, was forty feet deep.

And luck again camped on my trail, as we were following a narrow railroad through a wood, when two Americans beside the road opened a sack of bread and began to distribute it to passing soldiers. They handed me a loaf, which I took gratefully. That night my buddies and I had more for supper than the KPs dished out even if it was only bread.[6]

Camp that night was beside a small brook in a broad, wooded valley, where the long grass helped make us a bed. Just after retiring the Germans shelled us, the missiles hitting the ground a hundred yards back of us. Our guns replied. We were in front of them! A gas alarm came—a false alarm.

5

Bivouac and March

September 27 and 28

The gas alarm on the night of our arrival in these woods was the occasion of my putting on my gas mask for the first time when there might be a real danger. The shells and the cry of "gas" of course terrified us. After that first welcome to our bivouac, the Germans did not bother us but a time or two during our three days' stay at this place.

The first two days as well as most of the third were practically devoid of interest. To be sure they were ideal days for crapshooters and poker and blackjack players. My buddy and I spent most of our time reading our Testaments in a few feet of a crap game. They didn't bother us, nor we them. If they saw pleasure in what they were doing, it was none of our affair. Indeed, the army was a great place to learn how to attend to one's own business.

One of the few incidents that I remember in connection with our stay here was the jangling of some scores of canteens together, which produced noises very like cowbells as several details at intervals searched for and finally found water—a small spring—along the foot of the low hills near camp.

Most of the twenty-ninth, which was Sunday, was spent just as the two preceding days were, except in the afternoon I enjoyed a visit from a young fellow named Shinkle whose home was in Ohio. We had been friends in the 153rd. He was now in I Company.

An order to pack up ended Shinkle's visit. He hurried back to his company. This was the last I ever saw of this splendid fellow except a glimpse of him on the march. He was killed in battle a few weeks later.

In the bustle of packing up, a rifle shot rang out. We new men did not know what to make of it but soon learned the significance.

Some poor fellow had lost his nerve and shot himself through the foot.

At dark we marched out onto the road but we didn't hike—we merely stood in the road nearly all night. I must say that up to that time it was the worst night I had ever put over. And, of course, it rained; though I didn't have to say that for the benefits of the AEFers. They would know that without being told. We would move forward one hundred yards and stand for half an hour; then move ten yards and stand another thirty minutes. And the packs bore down heavily, believe me. I can't yet understand why we could not have at least sat down beside the road unless it was because, as we heard so often repeated, that a part of the army was run without brains. In this particular instance, the brains were not used.

I did stagger to the roadside one time and fell asleep in the rain. In the midst of a beautiful dream of home, a comrade called me. The outfit was on the move. Fifteen yards after I caught up, it stopped for another half-hour's stand. Did I feel like swearing?

September 30

An hour or so before day we really moved forward. Soon we were going at double time through the inky blackness. Can you imagine the fun of double-timing with full packs and stomachs not full? A few kilometers on our way and we came to a sure-enough ruined French village, the entire town being a mass of debris, few, if any, of the walls being higher than a man's head. These ruins, dimly discerned through the thick darkness, brought us face to face with war. I learned a few weeks later that the name of the village was Avocourt. It had a perfect right to be torn up, for the lines of battle had been on the hill a half mile north of the place from the beginning of trench warfare four years before up to September 26.

Immediately after passing through the town we halted with a jerk. Daybreak found us here changing from column of fours to single file so as to be able to pass the Rainbow transport train that was stuck in the mud on the slope just south of the old battle lines.[1] It was this stalled transport that had kept us on the road all night. But why, oh why, did we have to stand all the while in the middle of the road?

The trucks passed, we took up our double-timing again. The clouds hung low and heavy, so we were in no danger of being seen by enemy airplanes, for airmen of both armies usually took a holiday on occasions like this when the weather was bad. A mile or two down the road the pace began to tell. All semblance of military order began to disappear; the sides of the road were strewn with men who had fallen out; the marching columns resembled a routed mob more than anything else.

At length my own strength began to give way. Finding it harder and harder to keep my place in the line of march, eventually I began to drop behind, and although I exerted all my strength and strained every nerve and sinew I found it impossible to keep up. A strange company began to pass me, still I toiled on in hopes of at least keeping close to my outfit. Overtaking my buddy who was lagging behind, too, we tried to keep pace with the company nearest us, but the night in the rain, the lack of food, and the fierce pace had had their effect. Human endurance had its limit, and just as the road emerged from a small wood I stumbled to the roadside and fell heavily on a muddy bank. A merciful blackness shut out the world of war and slush and I seemed drifting through space. Sheer exhaustion held me thrall. It was the first and only time I ever fell out on any march. At length I became conscious of marching feet on the road and a gradual return of strength. I know not how long I lay there, but I suppose less than an hour. When I sat up, my eyes fell on a familiar form on the opposite side of the road—it was my buddy. The road was filled with stragglers trying to catch up with their outfits.

Twenty minutes later Shirey and I started in the hunt of M Company. Half a mile down the road we came upon Evans, who went with us. Every little while we found an M Company man who joined us until we had quite a crowd. At my suggestion we formed in column of squads and so marched in military formation. Our pace was a leisurely one and the march comfortable. We set the pace ourselves, see? The road was still filled with stragglers, and the farther we went the more prostrate figures were beside the road. The march had been too much for us—human endurance and even sheer will power could not stand the strain. Now we began passing M Company noncoms, veterans of many hikes as this, but they did not join us—the outfit was still ahead.

We came to a crossroads. By a singular chance no soldiers were in hailing distance. Which way had the company gone? We decided the most recent tracks led to the right, so we turned that way. Half a mile farther I found my corporal beside the road and knew that we were on the track of the fleet company and pressed on. At the edge of the woods was what had been a German machine-gun nest and near it a German cannon and other equipment with signs in the Boche language. We had reached the place where the enemy had made their first big stand after they were driven out of their trenches on September 26.[2] Did we have a creepy feeling?

In the deep woods we reached a crossroads, in the center of which stood Lieutenant McKee. We had found what was left of our company—about 20 percent of it. The boys were beneath the low trees on either side of the right-hand road. The good lieutenant took not the slightest note of our arrival, and we sought our comrades in the woods, for the first time since our induction being practically free from military restraint. Iron rations soon disappeared and we felt stronger.

Here beside the road was a soldier's grave. A Yank named Morris was buried there. He had been killed in the fighting that drove the Germans from these woods. The war was at hand now.

Two or three hours later when most of the stragglers had got in we were quite rested; we lined up and, taking the right-hand road, marched down into and across a deep valley and up to a broad flat-topped hill beyond. Then turning down a long straight road to the left we soon reached our camping ground. Pup tents were soon up and the cry "Crapshooters assemble" called a large part of the bivouackers to the great pastime.

Here on top of this hill the war might have been seen at its worst. Originally covered with big trees it must have been a beautiful place, but the crown prince's effort to take Verdun in 1916 had well nigh destroyed the forest. Broken, split, splintered stumps of varying heights covered the landscape, whose exposed wood grayed by weathering looked almost ghostlike in the twilight. Only here and there a whole tree was standing miraculously saved from the cannonading. The ground was pockmarked with all sizes of shell craters, covered here and there with treetops, while occasionally a weed or a poke stalk tried to hide nature's scars. Down near our camp the shell holes were fresh, some being sixteen feet across. Destruction was personified and from the quiet of the devastated region seemed to resound in tones of thunderous silence, "This is war."

Dark found me with my mess gear under my arm wandering up and down the road seeking M Company's kitchen. There were eight or ten parked here, but I could get no information as to the whereabouts of ours. Finally a kindhearted headquarters company man suggested that I fall in line at his kitchen and get chow, for said he, "We have so many men they won't know you." I got supper all right, plenty of it, good too, but I am sure the KPs knew I didn't belong to their company. I believe they smiled and gave me more than they did the others. I'll remember that supper when banquets have faded from my memory, and I am still grateful to headquarters company for the feed.

While eating this handout a machine gun not more than a hundred yards away opened fire. Likely a hostile airplane was near. Believe me, that gun made some racket. Almost simultaneously there was a great dash of light at a kitchen down the road. I thought the kitchen had exploded but guess I was mistaken. "German spy," said a voice at my elbow, "tipping them off as to our location." Perhaps it was. Scared silly I waited and expected German shells to begin falling in our midst but am glad that I was disappointed in my expectation.

October 1

Our kitchen arrived sometime during the night, and we had a good breakfast. Indeed our stay in these woods was not so uncomfortable. The first of golden October was spent quietly in camp, most of the time being devoted to my Testament.

All day long the sullen roar of artillery came from the north with an occasional explosion when a shell hit on the hill across the way where a field hospital was located. I remember that once, as I lay in our pup tent listening to the awful sounds and realizing with heavy heart that shortly we would enter the battle lines, I expressed the hope that we would emerge safely from the big drive. Shirey, my buddy, was not so enthusiastic. Said he, "If I don't get through, I have hopes of a better world than this." Poor fellow. He was mortally wounded at Romagne. God grant that the better world is his portion.

October 2

About two o'clock the crap games were interrupted long enough to call the company together and take subscriptions to the Liberty Loan then being raised. The money was to be taken from our salary and the bond sent home. I subscribed for a $100 bond, but that was the last I ever heard of it for I neither got the bond nor paid for it. Perhaps the sergeant had the list in his pocket when he was killed a few days later.

Then the names of all who could play any kind of an instrument were taken for the band. I can play an organ a bit, and my name was taken to go to Paris to learn to be a saxophone player. Luckily, I escaped that fate.

Just before dark I stood beside the road and watched the 126th Infantry pass on its way to enter battle. Some elements of this outfit actually took over a portion of the front line the next morning. Never shall I forget the sight of those brave men with the glint of battle on their set faces, silently marching past, some never to return, some to die a soldier's death within a few hours or days at most. All were to pass through the fiery furnace of modern warfare, an experience that would leave its imprint on body and mind alike for life.[3]

October 3

On the selfsame spot I stood an hour after daybreak the next morning and watched part of the Thirty-seventh Division that the 126th had relieved file by on their way to a place of rest. They were muddy, haggard, and most of them unshaven. All showed signs of utter weariness. Surely they had been through the mill. As a big fellow passed us Thirty-second men he sang out, "Better make your peace with your Jesus, fellows, before you go up there!" This was received in silence, for we all realized its truth.

About nine o'clock I made a trip to the spring down in the deep hollow near us. It was as fine a spring as I ever saw and as cold. There were German signs stuck up on the trees saying that the use of the water was "Verboten" (forbidden), but that did not deter us Yanks from drinking.

While at the spring I saw a German plane brought down. Five Allied planes attacked and sent it to the earth in flames. I could not help just a bit of pity for the aviator who must have been roasted. Months later I learned that this was seen by the soldier who lived nearest me in old Mississippi from the hill north of the spring. He was in the 127th; I had left him at [Camp] Pike.

As the twilight shadows gathered, our regiment lined up and marched away. It was our time to be fed into the bloody mill.

One is unable to describe that march, also to express his emotions. To be understood it must be experienced. Indeed, there are gaps in my memory at this early date as to the way we took and other incidents but there are residuary feelings that it was a time of horror. It will suffice to say that for most of us it was a season of constant prayer, the while we took our course in a general northwesterly direction and the thunder of battle became ever and ever nearer.

And the night was dark—lit only by the horrid glow from the battle lines. I remember once we stopped on a hard road under the lee of a thick border of low trees with an open field on the left. Flashes like lightning came from beyond the trees followed always by a roll of thunder, or rather I should say the flashes and roll were continuous, although the night was for a wonder cloudless. It was here that I for the first time became aware that each platoon had a stretcher along— gruesome reminder to timid hearts of the bloody business at hand.[4]

I remember some distance farther, down in a valley, we crossed a plank road. Thousands of Yanks have vivid recollections of this road. I wished we were to travel it, but it was not to be.

I remember in another valley—ah, how distant and dreamy it seems now, indeed, it had a touch of unreality then—a German shell fell just ahead of us and there was a cry, "First aid, K Company."

An instant later there was another shell and a flame that blazed a few minutes afterward. The old men were aghast at this, and I stood with heart aflutter until it died away. Maybe it was a new enemy device to locate us.

It seemed that our officers became rattled and did not know what to do. Shortly we went halfway up the steep slope of the hill to the north and halted. There were men already bivouacked there, and I stumbled over one of the tent ropes. The roar from within I was quick to placate.

After a time I was awakened from a pleasant slumber, and by the light of the cold stars, we climbed the hill and found ourselves on a road-level field. A hike was not distasteful, for we were quite chilly. When some of the boys fell into excavations about two feet in depth, with a shiver I took them to be new-made graves. Instead, as I learned later, they were the foxholes that saved the lives of many doughboys.

Halfway across the field, we were drawn up in squad column, battle array. Our whole battalion was present, but where we had lost the remainder of the regiment and when, I do not know.

Then we moved toward the flashes and noise at the woods on the far side of the plateau. I began to wonder if we were going over the top by night. But as we approached the woods, the flashes seemed to recede and, with a sigh of relief, I perceived that the front line was, like the end of the rainbow, still evanescent. Too, the battle activities were on the wane when we reached the brow of the hill and began to descend, and the circle of fire was still distant.

Once in the valley we went down it for some distance before we halted. It surely was long past midnight and we were all weary and our eyelids heavy. As I said, the night was far spent, the battle activities had waned, and the night was dark. To our right a deeper blackness indicated the presence of a steep hillside.

Then came the terse order, "There are already some men on the hillside but room enough for you too. Make yourselves as comfortable as you can without unrolling your packs." We stumbled partway up the hill, which indeed was a steep one, and, needless to say, were soon lost in the land of dreams.

6

In Support

When I awoke the world was on fire, at least that portion near me seemed to be. A barrage was going over and was being replied to. We were in the midst of the inferno. To the right, to the left, in front of me, behind me, above me the elements were livid with sparks and flame. Again I was experiencing that cracking, popping sound as of a giant fire magnified a thousand times like I had heard on the morning of the twenty-sixth, but this time it was not over the hill from us, it was near to us, all about us. However, the recumbent soldiers on the hillside were as yet inactive, unharmed.

In a moment all was clear to me. A new drive was on, and we were to be chief actors. Upon us, our bravery and fighting ability, the success of the endeavor largely depended.[1]

I sat up and looked around; few if any of my comrades gave signs of being awake. I watched the work of war go on. Down the valley immediately back of us, and over the hill, the landscape was aglow with flame; cannon flashes, flares, and bursting shells were everywhere, it seemed, save on our hillside. I felt that the front line was down that valley and that we would be called to make an attack presently. But while the inferno raged with noise and flashes of flame increasing, the moments dragged into hours, and finally dawn with laggard steps came.

Fog now shielded the landscape almost as effectively as night had done. Suddenly through the fog figures of men appeared in the valley to our rear. I thought at first they might be Germans, but as none of my comrades became alarmed, my fears soon departed. The figures grew in numbers and in distinctness, although they hardly seemed to move. Soon a battalion in battle formation stood out on the plain and came toward us. It was part of the 125th Infantry supporting an outfit that was going over the top. They tried to surmount the hill we were on and finding it too steep went around the steep slope. I heaved a sigh of relief when they passed, for I realized that I had a day or two more before the front line received my comrades and me. Too, I had learned that the front line was beyond the hill instead of down the valley. This came home to us soon when two big shells screamed over us and buried themselves in the valley beyond.

About eight o'clock, the troops who had reached the hillside before us up and marched around the hillside, leaving us to hold the position; this was a good sign that all was going well for us up ahead. These troops were the First Battalion of my own regiment.

Shortly after, I went for a canteen of water to a good spring in the valley, then I went on an exploring trip. I must admit that the pangs of hunger were largely responsible for this. As luck would have it I soon espied some men coming from the right with either a loaf of bread or a can of corned beef. Having all to gain and nothing to lose, I followed the back track and soon came upon a Ninety-first Division kitchen. Someone was giving away the supplies, and just as I appeared they pounced upon the last box, which was filled with corned beef. It went like hotcakes. Finally someone said, "This is the last one."[2] Immediately, a wild scramble ensued, a dozen men tussling for the tin, and I looked for a free-for-all fight to begin any moment. It must have been instinct that just at this instant prompted me to reach into the box to see for sure if it was the last one, in spite of the fact that the whole bunch might have fallen on top of me in their struggles. It happened that it wasn't the last by one, and I helped myself to a ten-pound can of "corn-wully" and walked away while the uproar over the other can continued.[3] Although it was a law of the army to respect the rights of a soldier when in possession of an article, I did not tarry long. What I mean by respecting the rights of an owner is that nothing would be taken from an individual by force, but that did not prevent its being stolen from him once his back was turned.

Back with the outfit I called my best friends, and we had a feast. Two or three uninvited ones came, but I did not have the heart to drive them away. The feast was only hardtack and corned beef, but to a hungry man it was hot biscuit and fried chicken. Hunger was for a moment appeased and part of the meat left for another time.

About two o'clock we followed the First Battalion. Once well around the hillside, the Boche began shelling us, and for the first time I lay prone to escape the shell splinters. We halted on a wooded slope facing the front and found places to spend the night among the undergrowth. We unrolled our packs, made ourselves good beds, and then lay down to listen to the big shells coursing by the dozens above us; both sides were firing over our heads. A chow detail that returned late in the afternoon frightened almost out of their wits brought tales astounding of sudden death and narrow escape in the valley we had just quitted two miles in our rear.

Hughes, Shirey, Evans, and I enjoyed another feast among the bushes just before the chow came. My can of corned beef was responsible for this too. So we four went to bed without the aching void so familiar before this and so many, many times afterward.

A couple of dead men and a dead horse on the roadside below us did not increase our morale, neither did a field full of shell holes in plain view just north of us inspirit us.

Just at dark the whole outfit took a spell of sneezing. A single shell loaded with sneeze gas exploded at the foot of the hill caused this. It was really funny how the gas gradually spread over the company area, each man beginning to sneeze as though he liked it as the gas got to him.

October 5

Early in the morning before the fog had cleared away, we moved about a kilometer and took position in foxholes vacated by another outfit the night before. Here we spent a terrible day, near the summit, on the reverse slope of a high hill.[4]

Hardly had we got into position when the Germans welcomed us by sending over a couple of big shells at the same time that shrieked like dozens of lost souls just a few feet over our heads and exploded with awful reports on the hill far beyond. Judging from their reports they seemed to be about forty-inch shells, though I guess they were only ten- or twelve-inch affairs. A dozen times during the day this was repeated, sometimes three salvos being fired. Each time I was scared silly but was otherwise unharmed.[5]

About eight o'clock I saw my first military funeral. The chow detail had just arrived and I was eating my breakfast when suddenly the fog lifted, allowing me to get a glimpse of the deep narrow valley just below us, where I saw two men digging away in a shell hole. Soon they stopped and went into a frame house across the road from the scene of their labors. They returned bearing between them a long board on which was a rigid figure clad in olive drab. The shell hole reached, the board was tilted and the corpse rolled off and into the improvised grave. A repetition of this and a second corpse lay beside the first. The grave was filled and the funeral was over.

This morning I saw my first Germans in the Meuse-Argonne, but they were prisoners. Of course when we arrived we asked our adjutant if we were going over the top. He, a brave and kind man, replied, "If the 127th up ahead of us does what is expected of it, we won't. If it fails we'll go in, relieve it, and make an advance." I fondly hoped it would act well its part, little knowing that I had a cousin up there.

An hour later we had proof that it was functioning well. There was a commotion down in the valley to our right. Straining my eyes to peer through the fog, I saw a hundred gray-green figures under the chaperonage of a few Yanks. About the time the fog lifted, seventy-five or eighty came around the hill to the left, then came half a hundred directly over the hill and right by us. They were all in high spirits and kept saying, "La guerre fini!" Truly for them the war was over.

I was surprised at their appearance. I expected to see bewhiskered individuals who looked more like bears than humans; instead I saw a bunch of healthy, well-fed, clean-shaven boys about our own age, who probably had the advantage in looks, unless some Americans of foreign birth had been weeded out of our outfit.

About eleven o'clock occurred one of the funniest incidents in my army career, and it wasn't funny either, and it happened in less time than it takes to tell it. With me in the foxhole were Shirey and Campbell, an "old" man from Texas. I was standing up reaching for some object on the surface of the ground when suddenly there was a concussion. I felt it and got down. For the life of me I can't remember hearing an explosion, but there must have been one. Then at the cry of "Gas!" we went into our gas masks. Almost instantly I caught sight of smoke arising about ten feet from us. Remembering tales of Civil War days when a bomb lay and smoked a while before exploding, I awaited in terror the explosion that I foolishly thought imminent, for I did not know then that World War shells always exploded when they hit or waited for something to give them an excuse to explode by hitting them or picking them up and dropping them on the ground or into the fire. So there I sat, every nerve rigid, looking to be blown into smithereens any moment. The suspense was awful, but nothing happened save an increase in the volume of smoke.

All at once Campbell pulled off his mask and began to laugh. Horrors, had the strain run him crazy, or was it a new gas that made its victims insane? Then Shirey pulled off his mask and the two laughed together. Now I knew it was a new gas; would it get me too? Then both the boys turned their attention to me, laughing and talking in turn. I didn't hear what they said, and they set themselves to getting off my mask. Great heavens! It was not enough to endure the horrors of war, and now I was at the mercy of a couple of lunatics who would pull off my mask and expose me to the gas and in a moment I would be raving also. I fought back with desperation; I would protect myself as long as I could. Then they tried new tactics. Campbell put his mouth close to my ear and shouted, "'Tain't gas." Convinced at length of his sanity, I pulled off my mask; there was not a whiff of gas in the air. I peeped out at the supposed shell and was just in time to see a man extinguish a burning pack. There had been but one shell and a fragment had hit a flare in his pack and set it on fire. The danger over, I joined my comrades in a hearty but nervous laugh.

Then I got up and looked around. The shell had made a direct hit on a telephone pole thirty feet distant and had broken it in two. The men on the other side of the post fared much worse than we. One of them was fatally hurt, one seriously, and three slightly.

In the afternoon my comrade Evans had a gruesome experience. He was sitting in his foxhole with his head just above the bank when he heard a shell and ducked quickly forward. When he leaned back again, he felt something soft and warm against the back of his head. It was part of the digestive organs of a corporal who had occupied the next hole. The shell had made a direct hit, blowing the corporal to bits and killing his two companions.

In all, the battle deaths of my own M Company that day, the fateful fifth of October, numbered five. One of them was jolly Frank Morgan, who had brightened the hours on our trip by truck to the front. He had found a soldier's grave before he reached the front line.

It was in this narrow valley that the major of our First Battalion had been killed along with his adjutant by an all but spent shell the day before.

Just before dark a chow detail from D Company passed us bound for the front lines. One member of this was grayed about the temples. He was sixty-six years old and unafraid. Almost the whole regiment knew him as "Dad" after the Armistice. And to think we had millions of husky young fellows back at home in their early thirties who deemed themselves too old to fight.

We slept in the foxhole but not all night, for there was other work to do.

7

In the Front Line

About 3:00 a.m. we were awakened and ordered to roll packs, which we did in the darkness. Setting out around the hill to the left, we headed toward the front. It was a bad march of three miles as we wound about quite a bit. Believe me, it was some dark too. I remember that we followed an insulated telephone wire laid along the ground for some distance and that once, when a German starlight shell blazed above the low woods not more than a quarter of a mile distant, we stood stock still.

Strange how an outfit like this at such a time and place killed time on the march. There was need of much caution in keeping together, in keeping the right path, and in not letting the enemy discover us. Just before dawn we went silently down a steep bank, across a ravine, and out into an open field. Drawn up there was another outfit—part of our First Battalion, which with muffled orders silently moved away on our back track. I cannot but marvel at the safety I felt that morning when I was the closest to the Germans I had ever been.

At dawn, nay, God's light was resplendent even when we betook ourselves to the ravine and deployed up and down it. I stopped a moment to speak to Hughes, and Flynn our platoon sergeant came along and put me on guard. There was no firing, and everything in our sector was as quiet as the grave. I noticed that Flynn gave me my orders in a whisper. This put me to studying and I asked him, "Where is the front line?" and added as the thought struck me, "Is this it?" He answered, "Yes," and a moment later, "The Germans are probably just over the hill," which was one hundred and fifty yards away.

Shortly, Steen, my corporal, called me and directed me to shift up the gully to my own squad. So another guard was placed and I went to my proper place, where I helped hold the line for two days. This ravine that served for a front-line trench was about ten feet wide and five deep; it was not straight at this particular place but was nearly so. Where I was the bottom was dry, but in the platoon area there was a good spring and below it, of course, a small brooklet. Back of us rose a steep bluff from the ravine to the height of fifty feet, and it was well wooded. In front of us was a slight fringe of trees down the bank of the ditch, and beyond was an open field sloping up gracefully and uniformly to the crest of the low ridge one hundred and fifty yards away where there were a few pines and other bushes. Just back of those we imagined the Germans to be. In the background could be seen a higher hill. As regards military matters, I will say that this position we occupied was the right side of the salient that may be seen on a battle map of that day just to the west of Gesnes. A day or two previous the Ninety-first Division had been withdrawn from this area and after our stay of two days returned to relieve us.

My, how still that Sunday morning was! Only desultory firing at a distance told of war still in progress. Conversation was scanty and then in whispers or an undertone. And there was nothing to do but wait. At last I was in the front line. If I could only get back home now what stories of war a hardened veteran could tell, and really I thought I was a veteran.

About 10:00 a.m. I was horrified to see an officer walking down the bank of the ravine fully exposed to the enemy and saying in stentorian tones, "Don't be shooting out across here. We are going to send out a patrol." Shortly I was aroused from my Testament reading by a squad mate remarking, "Doesn't that beat you?" I asked, "What?" Another replied, "They just walked right over the top."

It was the patrol. I had missed seeing it go, but I didn't miss hearing a machine gun cut loose and then seeing a Yank evidently wounded in the arm run back over the hill and make for the ravine. A moment later a real sprinter appeared. Our boys howled with delight when he made it safely to the ditch. The other three men in the patrol did not return.

When the man passed me on his way to report I asked him what they had found out. He was of foreign birth, scared almost to death and out of breath, so I learned nothing but that they did run into a machine-gun nest. I don't believe I ever saw anyone in worse fix from fear than this man was, for it seemed that every muscle of his body was twitching spasmodically and spots chased each other over his face. It seemed a pity to put these brave men through this just to learn where the hostile lines were, but it was one of war's requisitions.

After the patrol, quietness reigned again. I could not but think of still Sabbath mornings like this in quiet country and small towns and the crowds of worshipers who would throng the churches over all the vast land of America in a few hours and the prayers that would be offered for the nation's defenders. Once as I was reading, a little Catholic stopped before me and said, "While you are praying, remember and ask for peace and a return to the States by Christmas."

Two o'clock and all was as quiet as the grave in our sector. Crap-shooters were not at their pastime that day; those soldiers not reading their Testaments or on guard were asleep.

Three-thirty and the serenity was gone. The Germans were shelling us. Oh, but it was terrible! I took refuge in a small place dug out of the bank, but the protection was more imaginary than real. Bang! bang! bang! went the shells all around us, who expected each moment to be blown into bits. At the cry of "Gas!" we donned our masks. Bits of earth fell over me and around me, and pieces of stone blown up by the bursting shells hit my helmet with a metallic thud numbers of times.

This nerve-racking performance kept up for a half-hour. Finally, the squad guard who had been bravely holding forth over time called for his relief. The man who was supposed to relieve him did not stir, so I volunteered to take his place. The platoon sergeant almost immediately called down the line to know if we were watching. It was with much pride I returned the answer, "Watching." Three minutes later the barrage ceased. Instantly the Yanks were on their feet, bayonets fixed, and everything put into readiness to repel the attack we thought imminent. And it would have been a lively time if they had come, but they didn't.

Down to the right, rifles began to pop. Like a summer shower there were a few shots now and then, gradually increasing in number until there was a perfect roar. This lasted about ten minutes, and then the volume of noise began to decrease, dying away to a few desultory shots and then silence. That is all I know of what happened to our right, as it was out of sight. I have always believed that

that the war was soon to cease and no excitement except hiding from hostile airplanes that came over once in a while.

I salvaged a good helmet where a corporal and his whole squad had been killed by a single shell. I hated to wear a dead man's helmet but hated worse to become a dead man for lack of one. Then too such equipment was picked up and reissued to the boys anyway, so what was the difference?

May I tell you of an experience meeting I attended that afternoon at the Harness Lodge? There was a small log cabin near our bivouac built by the Germans and used by them as a storehouse for saddles and harness. It was about the size of a Mississippi cotton pen, and one corner of it had been splintered by a Boche shell. I shall refer to it as the Harness Lodge. The phrase came into my mind as I was jotting down my whereabouts that day in my Book of Proverbs. Thither a dozen Yanks had resorted to escape a sudden shower that drifted over the battlefield. I managed to get hold of a week-old copy of the Paris edition of the *Daily Mail* and was devouring its news— my first contact with the outside world in a couple of weeks—when I became aware of someone speaking.

"Yes, sir, I prayed while I was up there and am not ashamed of it," said the voice. I looked up and beheld a tall portly American of German descent who spoke good English and was by religion a Lutheran.

Another husky fellow said, "Yes, and I prayed not only for myself but for the others too."

A little Catholic spoke up, "I guess I was selfish; I prayed only for myself."

And so on around the crowd, each man telling of his reliance on prayer and God's wonderful goodness and protection to him. Only one man said he had not prayed. Said he, "I never thought of it."

Dreary dusk found a comrade named Kerr and me comfortably ensconced on a bed made of German saddles and harness in the big hut and that, too, in violation of orders.

But wait a minute. If I hadn't disregarded orders, you might be reading Zane Grey or Curwood, the chances are you would not be reading this because for our evening's entertainment and to prevent army life from getting monotonous, the Germans shelled us.[3] A shell fell ten feet from where I would have been if I hadn't disobeyed

the enemy counterattacked at the base of the salient with the intention of cutting us off and that they were foiled in their attempt.

Several casualties resulted to M Company from the barrage. A runner named Barrett was killed in a singular manner. He was lying on a shelf of the ditch and a shell passed a foot or two above him and exploded against the opposite bank. Though he was not hit by the shell and his body bore no evidence of wounds, it put his name on M Company's Honor Roll.

That night I was put on guard in no-man's-land with an Arkansawyer named Berry for my pal. This was the first guard duty I had ever done except that day in the ditch and a time or two on the train in the U.S.A. One of the men we relieved said that he thought he had heard a man cough about fifty yards from us. Did it put us on our mettle? Then too the German guards were just back of the pines on the crest of the ridge and the flares they sent up put us in full view of the enemy if we should move while they glowed, so there was no chance for us to get lonesome. Must say I had a delightful sleep after the guard duty.

October 7

A loud explosion awakened me. It was dawn and the Germans were shelling us. It was a horrible awakening, but I had almost got used to the shelling. Still, they were falling extremely close: on the bluff above me, out in no-man's-land, and down the ravine. One of them so hurt Brisendine, a member of my platoon, that he died before the boys got him to the first-aid station. Corporal Moon was wounded also. They were hit not a dozen yards from me. And yet I dozed off to sleep again.

The day passed similarly to the one previous except there was no afternoon barrage. However, I really believe that the wicked crack of the German rifle bullets just over our heads came oftener and made it hazardous to poke our heads above the ravine bank.

And before I forget it, I will say that I learned afterward that the German first line was on the second hill and that those of their forces on the ridge we watched were the outposts or sentinels. However, it wasn't any less dangerous because the enemy from the second hill could easily put a bullet over our trench.

In the afternoon each man was served with two doughnuts. As you remember, Salvation Army lasses were famous for their doughnuts and I suppose cooked these, but doughboys brought them to me. They were the only doughnuts I saw in the forty-seven days in the Meuse-Argonne.

At twilight a slow French rain set in. I was snug in a place I had dug out of the bank, as were most of the boys. My hour's guard was with Lowers of West Virginia. I wonder if the reader, if not an ex-service man, can halfway realize what a hardship this was as we lay prone on the wet ground with the cold raindrops pattering on our helmets, which glistened over and anon in the glow of German starlight shells.

8

In the Harness Lodge Woods

An hour before dawn, leaving one squad from each platoon to hold the lines until the relief arrived, we set out toward the rear. Half a mile on our way we met an element of the Ninety-first Division going up to take the position we had held for two days. They were just a trifle late, and it was dawn when the line was taken over by them.[1]

I have a vivid recollection of a bawling-out by my platoon sergeant as we were surmounting a high hill with the mud ankle-deep and us rain-soaked. I was so enervated that I couldn't keep up, try as hard as I might. It really looks to me that he ought to have known I would get away from the front as quickly as I could and if I didn't it was because I couldn't. Indeed, I had so little pep left that I didn't even resent what the sergeant said.

I caught up in time to rest with the platoon on that fateful hill where we had spent October 5. Two days ago we had left only our own dead there; now there were twenty-five little crosses at one huge grave on the hillside. Death's harvest had been abundant since we left here.[2]

Within a few feet of the grave I lay back on my pack and was just that soon asleep. A fellow is far spent when he can go to sleep by closing his eyes, but it is often thus with a soldier. When the march was resumed, I forgot my helmet; I had used it as my pillow.

Daylight found us traversing a wood along a road that had not been there when the war began. We turned to the left and dispersed among the bushes. A miserable day was spent, for we were wet, cold, and hungry. No fire could be permitted, so we shivered most of the livelong day. The rain had ceased, but the sun broke through the clouds only at rare intervals and the wind was raw. There was no pleasure to be seen except through trying to believe an idle rumor the enemy counterattacked at the base of the salient with the intention of cutting us off and that they were foiled in their attempt.

Several casualties resulted to M Company from the barrage. A runner named Barrett was killed in a singular manner. He was lying on a shelf of the ditch and a shell passed a foot or two above him and exploded against the opposite bank. Though he was not hit by the shell and his body bore no evidence of wounds, it put his name on M Company's Honor Roll.

That night I was put on guard in no-man's-land with an Arkansawyer named Berry for my pal. This was the first guard duty I had ever done except that day in the ditch and a time or two on the train in the U.S.A. One of the men we relieved said that he thought he had heard a man cough about fifty yards from us. Did it put us on our mettle? Then too the German guards were just back of the pines on the crest of the ridge and the flares they sent up put us in full view of the enemy if we should move while they glowed, so there was no chance for us to get lonesome. Must say I had a delightful sleep after the guard duty.

October 7

A loud explosion awakened me. It was dawn and the Germans were shelling us. It was a horrible awakening, but I had almost got used to the shelling. Still, they were falling extremely close: on the bluff above me, out in no-man's-land, and down the ravine. One of them so hurt Brisendine, a member of my platoon, that he died before the boys got him to the first-aid station. Corporal Moon was wounded also. They were hit not a dozen yards from me. And yet I dozed off to sleep again.

The day passed similarly to the one previous except there was no afternoon barrage. However, I really believe that the wicked crack of the German rifle bullets just over our heads came oftener and made it hazardous to poke our heads above the ravine bank.

And before I forget it, I will say that I learned afterward that the German first line was on the second hill and that those of their forces on the ridge we watched were the outposts or sentinels. However, it wasn't any less dangerous because the enemy from the second hill could easily put a bullet over our trench.

In the afternoon each man was served with two doughnuts. As you remember, Salvation Army lasses were famous for their doughnuts and I suppose cooked these, but doughboys brought them to me. They were the only doughnuts I saw in the forty-seven days in the Meuse-Argonne.

At twilight a slow French rain set in. I was snug in a place I had dug out of the bank, as were most of the boys. My hour's guard was with Lowers of West Virginia. I wonder if the reader, if not an ex-service man, can halfway realize what a hardship this was as we lay prone on the wet ground with the cold raindrops pattering on our helmets, which glistened over and anon in the glow of German starlight shells.

8

In the Harness Lodge Woods

An hour before dawn, leaving one squad from each platoon to hold the lines until the relief arrived, we set out toward the rear. Half a mile on our way we met an element of the Ninety-first Division going up to take the position we had held for two days. They were just a trifle late, and it was dawn when the line was taken over by them.[1]

I have a vivid recollection of a bawling-out by my platoon sergeant as we were surmounting a high hill with the mud ankle-deep and us rain-soaked. I was so enervated that I couldn't keep up, try as hard as I might. It really looks to me that he ought to have known I would get away from the front as quickly as I could and if I didn't it was because I couldn't. Indeed, I had so little pep left that I didn't even resent what the sergeant said.

I caught up in time to rest with the platoon on that fateful hill where we had spent October 5. Two days ago we had left only our own dead there; now there were twenty-five little crosses at one huge grave on the hillside. Death's harvest had been abundant since we left here.[2]

Within a few feet of the grave I lay back on my pack and was just that soon asleep. A fellow is far spent when he can go to sleep by closing his eyes, but it is often thus with a soldier. When the march was resumed, I forgot my helmet; I had used it as my pillow.

Daylight found us traversing a wood along a road that had not been there when the war began. We turned to the left and dispersed among the bushes. A miserable day was spent, for we were wet, cold, and hungry. No fire could be permitted, so we shivered most of the livelong day. The rain had ceased, but the sun broke through the clouds only at rare intervals and the wind was raw. There was no pleasure to be seen except through trying to believe an idle rumor

49

that the war was soon to cease and no excitement except hiding from hostile airplanes that came over once in a while.

I salvaged a good helmet where a corporal and his whole squad had been killed by a single shell. I hated to wear a dead man's helmet but hated worse to become a dead man for lack of one. Then too such equipment was picked up and reissued to the boys anyway, so what was the difference?

May I tell you of an experience meeting I attended that afternoon at the Harness Lodge? There was a small log cabin near our bivouac built by the Germans and used by them as a storehouse for saddles and harness. It was about the size of a Mississippi cotton pen, and one corner of it had been splintered by a Boche shell. I shall refer to it as the Harness Lodge. The phrase came into my mind as I was jotting down my whereabouts that day in my Book of Proverbs. Thither a dozen Yanks had resorted to escape a sudden shower that drifted over the battlefield. I managed to get hold of a week-old copy of the Paris edition of the *Daily Mail* and was devouring its news— my first contact with the outside world in a couple of weeks—when I became aware of someone speaking.

"Yes, sir, I prayed while I was up there and am not ashamed of it," said the voice. I looked up and beheld a tall portly American of German descent who spoke good English and was by religion a Lutheran.

Another husky fellow said, "Yes, and I prayed not only for myself but for the others too."

A little Catholic spoke up, "I guess I was selfish; I prayed only for myself."

And so on around the crowd, each man telling of his reliance on prayer and God's wonderful goodness and protection to him. Only one man said he had not prayed. Said he, "I never thought of it."

Dreary dusk found a comrade named Kerr and me comfortably ensconced on a bed made of German saddles and harness in the big hut and that, too, in violation of orders.

But wait a minute. If I hadn't disregarded orders, you might be reading Zane Grey or Curwood, the chances are you would not be reading this because for our evening's entertainment and to prevent army life from getting monotonous, the Germans shelled us.[3] A shell fell ten feet from where I would have been if I hadn't disobeyed orders, exploded, and wounded a man twenty feet away in a direct line beyond where I was supposed to be. He was hit in the ankle and was away from us for months.

But I'll tell you that barrage wasn't funny. Whoppers fell all around us, and lots of them too. The screech of the shell and then the loud report of the explosion was enough to appall the stoutest heart. I expected every instant for a shell to hit the cabin and knock it into kindling wood, but luckily we escaped because we were shielded by the hand of Providence.

If I mistake not, the battalion miraculously escaped without a fatality, though there were many wounded, gassed, and shell-shocked. In fact, M Company lost about thirty men including the acting top and two other sergeants.

The story was told that over in L Company four men were occupying a deep shell hole. One of them had a hunch that he ought to get out of the hole. The others laughed at him, but the presentiment persisted and he announced that he was going if the others didn't. When he left, the others followed, and just as the last one got safely on the bank, a shell fell plump into the cavity they had just left.

October 9

This was almost a repetition of the previous day except that the sun shone more and that we had to be more particular about hiding from airplanes. I spent the day under the bushes and in the long grass with my squad but at night returned to the log cabin where Kerr and I took in Prather of West Virginia for a bunkie. For many, many days Prather was to be my close associate, and as I look back over my army experiences I find that he was about the only one that I was closely associated with on the front that was not killed or wounded. That evening the shells fell a little way down the hill from us and were not so numerous.

A gruesome experience was mine while in these woods. It came my turn to fill the squad's canteens, and I set out with others on a similar errand. At the eastern end of the woods ran a north-south road. Along it streamed men on various errands. Some were wounded going to the rear. I have a distinct recollection of a Fifth

Division corporal with blood dripping from his fingertips trudging along with a companion less seriously wounded.

Down in the valley nestled a once snug little village. It was Cierges, as I afterward learned. To the north the noise of battle made a constant din. It was reported that the 126th Infantry had taken an important hill that day.

We left the road and, passing some frame buildings, went down into a hollow. On the hillside beyond was a large pump and excellent water. A short distance to the left was a small clump of trees. It seemed that the other Yanks thought there was something of interest there, for their attention seemed to be drawn to the place. Sensing from their attention that there was some attraction I followed the crowd and discovered a spring in a dug-out place in the midst of the trees. Around the spring lay three dead Germans with features distorted and bloated. The sight filled me with loathing and disgust. Here had been a machine-gun nest, and the Boche gunners had stayed to the death. Brave must have been the Yanks who surrounded the nest and killed the gunners in an open field.

October 10

We had a bite to eat for breakfast and then packed up and started on a brisk hike. This was not unwelcome, for the air was chilly and Yanks wanted to leave no matter where they were. Indeed, the two chief questions that occupied the minds of Uncle Sam's boys in Europe were, "When do we eat?" and "Where do we go from here?"

Then too on this particular morning we might be going to the rear to rest up. We took the road I had traveled the afternoon before. When we should reach the road at the end of the woods, if we took the right it was the rear and rest for us; if we turned to the left it was back to the front with all that it entailed. I almost held my breath as we approached the road. We turned to the left.

9

North of Cierges

At the corner of the woodland we stopped and spaced the platoons. Then we moved northeastward across country, through a shallow valley. The weather was chilly, the sky clear, there was some frost, the sun had not yet risen. Now and then we saw a figure clad in olive drab on the ground. Some so closely simulated sleep that were it not for the frost on their clothing and hair one would think it was only a Yank asleep, but these were sleeping the last long sleep of the ages, for they had been slain a day or two previously when the Boche had been driven from these fields. Many a mother's heart would break when the news would be flashed to distant America.

We took position on a gentle declivity, the second one north of Cierges. Hardly had we arrived when a German shell near the top of the hill told us that the enemy had seen us come. Steen and three of us privates went to a place in the lee of a small clump of bushes on a hillside where a Yank was issuing equipment. We drew a Chauchat and several musette bags of ammunition. Returning to the squad, Steen asked me to be automatic rifleman, that is, to carry the Chauchat.

Here let me say that this implement of warfare, usually announced "sho-sho" by the soldiers, is a French automatic rifle and doesn't amount to much for fighting. Of course a "sho-sho" bullet will kill if it hits, but getting it to hit is the main thing, for it is not very dependable. Then too it jams much too often to suit me. I had the promise of instruction in its operation but received none except as to how to load it. An order to advance came too soon for any instruction. At 12:45 we went forward. An element of our division was making an attack on the front line, and we were moving up in support.

Hardly had we started when shells began falling near us. This was just an incident of a battle, and not minding them much I gave myself over to thought of the military glory of making an attack on the enemy. This for a moment thrilled me, and I watched with pride the battalion of Yanks that stretched over the landscape. Marching across the hills to the north of Cierges, to the left was the valley of the little river, Andon, down which the road ran, west of that rose low hills, an almost exact counterpart of those we were traversing.

At first the shells were not falling so close to us and we ignored them, but soon they were falling among us and things began to look serious and a little fear crept in and mixed itself with my military thrills. I glanced across the valley; another battalion was marching there, and shells were falling in their midst. Beautiful sight! Military grandeur! Two battalions advancing in parallel column unmindful of the storm of shells that were poured upon them. What matter if a few men did falter when a shell fell too close to them, the outfits as a whole kept on like the onward march of fate.

Now business began to pick up in our sector. Just to the left the earth boiled up at the feet of the sergeant of the next platoon. He fell to earth covered with dirt, and I was sure he was killed, but instantly he arose and led on. A moment later another shell fell as closely to him. He was down, and up, and on his way in less time than it takes to tell it. Thinks I, here is really a brave man.

The next instant the earth boiled up beside our corporal and most of the squad fell down while the earth that had been dislodged fell all over us. Gosh but it was a close call. Then firing ceased for a few moments and our path led down into a deep hollow where we were comparatively safe. Atop the next hill it began again with renewed fury—there was a perfect shower of shells, although they mostly fell ahead of us.

Then came the command to halt and lie down. I looked across the valley for the other battalion, but it was not to be seen. Doubtless it too was lying down. Then the terse command, which was quickly obeyed: "Dig in right where you are."

For a few minutes shells fell on the hillside in front of us, then ceased altogether. The meaning was clear—the advance had stopped. Whether the objective was obtained or not, I do not know. It seems almost a miracle that we should have gone a mile through that awful barrage without having a single man wounded much less killed, but such was the luck of M Company.

As soon as I had dug a hole large enough to be hidden in, I got in. There I stayed for the rest of the afternoon and slept, slept alone through the cold night with the earth for a couch and no covering save the canopy of heaven, while the cold stars kept their vigils over friend and foe alike.

October 11

I spent practically the entire day in the same little place with no diversion save reading my Testament. Broken clouds flecked the sky. When the sun shone it was quite pleasant; but when clouds prevailed it was too chilly to be comfortable. And the Germans to keep us scared and weaken our morale sent over a few shells every once in a while. The main track of these was directly over me. With the rush and roar of a railway train and the scream of a fire siren many times magnified, they would pass not ten feet overhead and explode in a slight depression not a hundred yards from me.

It seems that one might eventually get used to them, but not so. There was always the possibility that they would fall right at one and blow him into smithereens. And one night while here, I was asleep when all of a sudden came one of these hideous noises, louder than ever with a louder report and closer approach. When I opened my eyes the elements above me were shot through with flame. With the shriek, the explosion, and the fire, I thought my time had come, and it did almost, for my heart almost leaped out of my body and from the pain I thought surely it had caused one of the large arteries to burst. For weeks every time I was excited, which was very, very often, it pained me immensely.

And yet with all this talk one who has never experienced it cannot understand and realize how a soldier must suffer.

We had missed four meals in succession, consequently food would have been very welcome. It fell to the lot of our squad to be the chow detail, so late in the afternoon we left our position and wended our way back through ruined Cierges to a hospital atop the hill beyond, where we had not long to wait for the chow. I have a pleasant memory of Cierges because one of the best springs of water I ever saw was within a ruined house at the edge of the town. Here I quenched my thirst and filled my canteen for future use.

We would have hardly been human if we had not eaten just a bit of the chow before starting back, but Steen was in a hurry, so the return began soon. Although there was nothing whatever of army service we would more gladly have done than this, we found the return trip tiresome, for we were terribly weak from hunger, and rests were frequent and necessary. Night's sable mantle had descended long ere we reached the company. Of course we got our share of the supper, and there was enough for all, so with hunger appeased for the instant I went back to my earth bunk to sleep and to dream fitful dreams, to wake when the shells screamed over, to shiver with the cold and to contract rheumatism in my right knee and thigh.

The Hill South of Romagne

The hill south of Romagne was my home for three days, that is, two whole days and part of two more. At the time I was staying there I did not know that there was such a place as Romagne, and if I had, I had no reason whatever to know that it was anywhere near. I have already told you of the incidents of part of my stay there and will now proceed with the record of October 12.

On the tenth, one of the squad had disappeared, none of us knew when or why but another man unattached to any squad had taken his place. On the eleventh one of the men found out that he had become a victim of mustard gas and went to the hospital; on the morning of the twelfth, his buddy followed for the same reason.

Prather, a West Virginian who lived in the next foxhole to mine, invited me over to share his home with him so that we could talk when we wished. It involved the labor of enlarging the excavation, and we had just begun this when Flynn, the platoon sergeant, put a stop to it by saying that quite likely we would move soon. As the day wore on and we did not move, Prather worked at the excavation at intervals and by night had a comfortable two-man burrow.

My rheumatism pained me so severely that several times during the day I had to get up and walk around, disregarding the danger of shells and flying bullets that ever and anon whizzed past. Guess I was foolish not to go to the hospital but thought I would stay as long as I could.

Just before dark Prather suggested that, as we were not going to move, I bunk with him. We salvaged some blankets from the battle-field and fixed a good bed. Then as the clouds presaged rain, I stretched my shelter half over the burrow. And I lied glibly to Flynn when he questioned me about a violation of orders not to unroll packs. He probably intended to bawl me out. The poor fellow had been so nervous for several days that the least thing would throw him into a furor. So to keep the man from raving about nothing I told him the shelter half had been salvaged along with the blankets. The thing I hate worst about the incident is that Flynn did not sur-vive the drive and I cannot tell him better. However, my pack with the exception of that article was ready to ride at a moment's notice, and I can't still see the sense of lugging the thing around if it were not going to be used, though I don't criticize the sergeant as he was merely enforcing the orders of higher-ups.

My wisdom in stretching the shelter half was soon evident. With night came rain and by the time I went on gas guard it was coming down briskly. I spent a lonely hour with my head above the shelter half looking out over the dreary landscape with the raindrops gently tapping on my helmet. But we had a cozy bed, and as there was prac-tically no shelling we had a good night's rest. I could not but pity the poor fellows all around us who lay all night in the drenching rain with no protection whatever. Perhaps it would have been better for them to have disobeyed orders and to have lied about a shelter half.

It was a boyish idiosyncrasy, I know, but I used to wonder if at sun-set in cemeteries of our land the spirits of the departed would not sometimes come out of their graves, seat themselves on the mounds or the tombstones, and converse with each other, and then as twi-light deepened seek again the repose of their earthy beds. Here on this gory field I saw and helped enact this scene almost to a "T." The only difference was that the actors were not spirits but flesh and blood. It seems strange yet how the fellows would, late in the after-noon, especially here on this hill, climb out of their burrows and come over and chat with me, even perfect strangers did so, telling me of their hopes and fears and spiritual condition, and how they had read their Testaments and prayed and then asked what further they should do, just as though I were their chaplain or their confessor. I've had as high as a dozen come to me one after the other in one afternoon and why they came to me rather than someone else I can't say, but I gave them all the encouragement I could and always advised them to keep praying. It did me good to see the light of new courage in many faces as the soldier went back to his burrow for a long terrible night. I could not cheer all, however, although I tried ever so hard and I am sure some souls went into eternity with my words of comfort as their last sounds of spiritual advice. God grant that they are at rest.

October 13

At the first streak of day, big Otto McKinley absentmindedly set out in search of a match to light his cigarette. He lit the cigarette, the Germans saw the light, and we were shelled forthwith as a result. McKinley was slightly hurt and possibly others; Prather and I were badly scared. The shells fell with a vengeance, some afar and some near. The last one fell just a few yards off, and a large fragment whizzed not more than two feet above our heads and a huge something fell onto our shelter half and caused it to sag. In terror we both sprang to our feet only to find that it was Prather's pack cut almost in two by the shell fragment. He had little left that was worth keeping.

About 9:00 a.m. we had orders to move to the rear by the infiltration process, that is, one or two at a time. Because Prather and I waited for orders to start, Flynn made us wait until the rest of the platoon had gone. I failed to see any punishment to this as I had much rather have been the last to go than the first, for I was then reasonably safe from shells as the others hadn't been shelled.

The entire landscape between the position we left and our new one was dotted with still figures clad in the olive drab uniform. One figure with hands clasped in prayer will linger indelibly in my memory. This was the inspiration of my poem, "A Soldier in Prayer." Three of our men had been buried alive in their foxhole by a single shell. I don't know that we had other battle deaths on the hill.

The position we took a kilometer to the rear was on a sloping hillside just in front of a battery of 75s and to the left of another.[1]

Prather and I dug in hard dry clay—a rarity. American shells were
falling on the hill above us just a kilometer too short to harm the
enemy. German shells were satanic enough, but it seemed to me
that American shells had just a bit more of the devil in them. Oh
yes, I know some of the officers have claimed that these were German shells from across the Meuse.[2] It seems to me that it would have
been impossible for Boche shells to have come from the southwest,
which was certainly the direction from which they hailed, so they
could only have been of American origin.

That afternoon I shaved for the first time in more than a week.
No, I didn't care to look spic and span, nor did I think our tour of
duty was ended. I felt that we were fixing to go over the top, and I
didn't want to be looking like a bear if I got killed.

In the next foxhole to mine was a medical officer attached to the
Fifth Division. When the American shells began falling again, he
ordered me to stop shaving until the shelling ceased.

10

Over the Top

Yes, I'll remember October 14 a long time. We went over the top.[1]

We were up before day and lined up to go back to the front. Steen told us that we were to make an attack. And we went back over the same ground we advanced over on the tenth, although we bore to the left. I don't know who started it, but the front was already in an uproar. Cannons boomed, shells shrieked and exploded, machine guns popped, and flares lighted up the darkness just preceding the dawn. It seemed that a lively scrap was now in progress and more in prospect. And while the din was in progress and we were taking our way to the jumping-off place, dawn drew on apace.

As we were going down a steep slope in squad column, Armstrong, a gallant fellow from Tennessee, just behind me, fell and cried, "First aid!" He had been hit by a piece of shrapnel. Cameron stopped to assist him, and four only of the squad kept on.

Going straight toward the thickest of the battle, where the din was the greatest, I tried to keep up my courage by singing, but somehow the song would not harmonize with the noise. Indeed, I could hardly hear myself and soon ceased singing.

And then at the crest of a hill we halted and lay down. In the dim light I could discern a barbed-wire entanglement and the company going through in single file. We had come to the German third line, the Kriemhilde Stellung, which they thought could not be taken. Evidently a brave detail of Yanks had cut a lane through the wire.

When it came our time to go on, Prather had to make the third attempt to rise as his pack overbalanced him. Flynn cursed him. I was horror stricken and could not repress the thought, "Isn't it terrible for him to be swearing this way and he to face a Maker so soon?"

Of course, we were all facing death, and I fully realized it but had hopes of coming through safely. For some days, however, the belief had been growing on me that Flynn would not survive the drive and that he knew it. I didn't know it at that time, but he had confided to his fellow noncoms the night before when told of the coming attack that the Boche had his number and that he would be a casualty on the morrow. His comrades tried to persuade him not to go into the battle, but he steadfastly refused to heed their advice. Truly, he was a brave man.

In single file, we came to the lane cut through the wire entanglement. Halfway through a machine gun opened upon us and we dropped to the ground. As I dropped I heard a bullet hit the wire on either side of me. A close call that! Through the wire, we found the company in shell holes on a bench of the hill toward the Germans. There daybreak found us subjected to a merciless shelling.

Several deeds of bravery and other incidents I must mention. One was a feat of my longtime friend Hughes. As company runner, he made two trips back through the lane in the wire while German shells were falling thickly there, but he went through the barrage four times unscathed. A call for another runner brought a response from Lloyd E. Brown, who set out briskly on his mission. I never saw him again. His name appears on M Company's Honor Roll with the date of his death given as October 13, which is an error as it was the fourteenth.

Ten feet from me was a six-foot jump-up of the hill. In this bank a small excavation had been dug. Thither an M Company man betook himself and ever and anon peeped out to see what he could see. He peeped once too often and an enemy sharpshooter took him between the eyes. A groan called my attention to him. He jumped down, ran a short distance, and dived headlong into a hole, kicking the air as he went. Soldiers nearby called for the first-aid man, but that worthy spent a moment in the hole with him and then went about his business. I knew by that that the man was dead.

And there was a great surge of concern in my breast when a big shell hit just below my area of vision and blew a Yank overcoat into the air and the thought came to me, What if that were little Evans' overcoat (it hit near where I knew him to be) and he is blown to pieces? How can I ever tell his parents? Luckily there had been no Yank in the coat when the shell hit.

Soon three men came up the hill, two of them carrying the third between them seated on a rifle. Evidently he was seriously wounded as his trousers leg had been slit and a bloody bandage indicated the hurt place, but he was coolly smoking a cigarette. If I mistake not, his leg was broken. His face looked familiar, and as he neared me I recognized Lieutenant Pelton, the company commander. He said to us: "Don't mind me. I am not hurt much. Give them the best you've got."

I hated to see our commander leave, as did all the other boys, for he was an efficient and popular officer. I learned later that his commission as captain reached him that day. I can't say that this is true but do know he deserved it.

Shortly the platoon commanders were called down the hill to the company post of command. When Flynn returned, he was the calmest I had seen him for days. He gave us the last order I ever heard him give; it was: "We make an advance at 8:30; it is now 8:22."

So the time had come that I had dreaded so long. The order was received in silence. I reflected, "I may have only eight minutes to live."

Perhaps you will wonder what one thought of at such a critical time. Well, there were many things, some flippant, some serious. It seemed a long eight minutes. I thought of home and loved ones, of my buddies on that battlefield, of my soul's condition, of the future, of food, of bullets, of victory, of death, of heaven. And with a smile I tried to see if I was any worse scared than I had been. My nerves had been strung at high tension for days, and especially that morning the shelling had put them at their highest, so I can't say the news scared me at all. When one has been looking over a dreary, bloody battlefield for days and expecting any minute for the scene to change and the Pearly Gate to be standing there, his nerves can't bear much more. The only effect of the terse announcement during the next few minutes was that I became a little bit chilly, that was all. I noted all the fellows near me and poor Shirey in particular. He had aged much since the drive began, and I felt that he too realized that he would be a battle casualty. It was the last time I ever saw him.

The moments ticked slowly away, and when the zero hour came, we went over the top.

But it was different from what I thought it would be. I expected us all to rise and start at the same time, but we didn't. There was a low embankment around the bench where we were located. A Yank went to the embankment and directed us when to go by squads. Two or three men would go, then when out of sight a squad. Finally, this man was beckoning to my squad, and, muttering to the other boys, "Well, I guess, we'd better go," I started forward. The other boys went alongside. When we came to our big, burly corporal he was in tears; he could not go, for he was wounded. So we three set out without a leader, but just as we were surmounting the embankment, Rake, the man on my left, stiffened and fell heavily. I thought almost flippantly, "Poor fellow, he is dead."

Then I looked to the front. Instead of a company marching gloriously as I had supposed I would see, the boys were all strung out over the hillside and in shell holes or prone on the ground and all banging away with their rifles, so I plunged into the first shell hole, which happened to be a very small one—it was made by a one-pounder shell—but a small place was better than none, so I began my part of the battle there. The boys laughed at me as long as I was with them, for they said I had my feet hidden and thought I was completely concealed from the enemy.

To my great surprise, down in the valley directly ahead of us was a large village. It was Romagne-sous-Montfaucon, but I did not know it for some days. The main thing now was not what place it was but how to get the Germans out of it.

I turned my attention to my Chauchat. I had not yet been taught how to shoot it, but evidently it would shoot, so, loading it, I set it down as it should have been and began trying to work the thing. I tried this thing and then that and finally I accidentally let loose a contraption and the thing went "Bam!" I looked to see if it was pointed toward the Germans and it was, so I had not hit any of our men. It was set on single shot, and though I have since wished it had been on automatic, perhaps it was lucky that it wasn't.

Then I began firing at the Germans, aiming as best I could with the old blunderbuss. Soon it jammed, but I had it working again in a jiffy. This happened again and again and finally, when I had shot about thirty rounds, was losing some of my fear, and beginning to enjoy it, Cameron stuck his head over the embankment and yelled, "Quit shooting with that Chauchat."

So here I was in the midst of a battle with orders not to shoot. I was loath to quit but was afraid not to, for I did not know who had told him to tell me to quit. I had shot at the town and the woods to the left and the field beyond but could have no definite aim and do not know whether I hit anyone or not. I had a close call there, for a bullet kicked up the earth just beneath my left knee, which at the time was about six inches aboveground. As I had nothing to do, I looked around for better protection. Directly in my front was a large shell hole. I loaded up my belongings and made a dash for it, arriving safely. And then fool-like I stuck my head out to watch the happenings. My, how I did wish for a good old Springfield, and through my thoughts came running the words, "And this is a battle, and this is a battle," and "I'm a participant in a battle."

The rifle fire kept up, and still the bullets whizzed, and the big guns boomed, and the shells crashed. After an hour of it, I began to wonder if we would have to say we had failed in our attack and wait until night to withdraw. And looking around I saw to my right a still, prone figure with a noncom's belt on. It was poor Flynn. He had gone over the top bravely at the head of the platoon at exactly 8:30; at 8:31 he was as dead as a doornail with a bullet squarely between his eyes and another through his right knee. In the next shell hole to my left was a wounded boy, the bloodiest man I have ever seen, I think. A bullet had hit his forehead and circled around his head, thus cutting a long gash. I thought of going over to his assistance but decided not to as he was doing fairly well it seemed and the bullets were flying thick and fast.

I looked back up the hill and saw Rake's rifle wiggling about, so I decided he was not dead and perhaps not seriously wounded. It happened that the bullet that laid him flat on the ground had only grazed the side of his head and raised a knot without cutting the skin, though it went through his helmet and mess kit. I had thought of running and getting his Springfield before I saw him using it.

But of all fools, the worst was the man who jumped out of a shell hole and risked the flying bullets merely to light his cigarette.

I looked toward the hill to the left. Over a little of the hill came some fifty gray-green figures waving white handkerchiefs. Immediately a murmur went along our hillside, "Don't shoot; they're giving up." And I watched them until they were taken in tow by some Yanks who rose out of shell holes in their paths, and not a one of them had been hit by either bullet or fragment of a shell.

But even though these Germans had surrendered, I was still afraid that the battle would last until night. Finally I looked far to the southwest and there on the skyline of the hill was a figure of a man standing out in bold relief. A few moments later there were two or three of them, and every few moments when I looked back there were more. My attention was divided between them and some Germans who darted back and forth behind a stone wall in the edge of the town. Bullets knocked up bits of stone from its top, and I wished to share in the sport. Finally a whole battalion of Yanks had come over the hill to the southwest and were marching up the country as if to aid us but had a long way to come and their pace was slow.

Just in front of me was a larger shell hole and beside it lay a still figure, which looked quite familiar. I reasoned he must be dead or he would have got into the shell hole, but as I looked the dead came to life, turned his head, and seeing me winked at me. Did you ever have a dead man wink at you? It almost gave me that impression, though he was much alive and afterward became my buddy. His name was Banholzer.

Presently, as the Yanks across the way, who happened to be the Second Battalion of our regiment, advanced, a German broke from the thicket atop the hill opposite us. Perhaps he intended to warn his comrades in the village that they were in danger of being surrounded. Guns popped at him and I grabbed my Chauchat with the same feeling and zest a hunter experiences when he sees a squirrel. Before I could shoot, the Hun had dived into a shell hole.

Victory

It seemed strange to me that the Second Battalion could march on so complacently, as it appeared to me that they were not meeting a great deal of opposition. At length I sensed that fewer bullets were flying in my vicinity. Perhaps the two elements were getting what one had formerly, or the Germans were turning their attention to the newcomers. As the bullets were not whistling so briskly, I took a notion to get down abreast the foremost boys so I could use my gat and not hit a Yank. A series of runs from shell hole to shell hole soon brought me there, but now a little hill was in my way. I was suggesting to my comrades that we negotiate the distance when of all horrors two American shells whizzed over and landed there. German shells were bad but those were worse, and we scampered back up the hill to get away from others that might follow, which soon happened. I don't remember running from a German shell, but I did from our own and made good time, too.

A flare was sent up and the big guns lifted and two or three salvos struck the town and tore great holes in the houses and roofs right before our eyes.

Meantime the Yanks on the opposite hill had come abreast of us. Two hundred Germans came out of the town and gave up to them, a few escaped over the hill, and the battle was over. Doubtless they were well-nigh surrounded as the 125th Infantry had attacked on the right of the town, we had made a frontal attack, and the Second Battalion had gone in to the left, so they could do nothing less than run or give up.

A calm ensued, and we set to work gathering up our wounded. I helped with the bloody boy I mentioned before. Some of us happening to have some bread along took a light luncheon, and then the battalion moved forward. Ogden led the platoon, now much depleted. Abreast the Second Battalion we passed through and encompassed the town, I being in the first wave. I understand a company or two of the 125th were sent in to mop up the town while we went on and established a line beyond it. After crossing the bridge into the town, my platoon was drawn back and advanced down the right bank of the stream. At a narrow-gauge railroad in the woods we halted.

All was quiet along the Andon, and the Boche seemed far away, so driven by thirst I went to a large house about one hundred yards to the right and at the foot of the bluff. I failed to find water, but a 125th Regiment captain had established his post of command there. He was in an extremely good humor, doubtless on account of the victory, and told me to tell my commanding officer to form a liaison with his command. Going back to my outfit I ran across our acting top, a fellow Short by name and otherwise. I reported the matter to him and got a bawling out for my pains.

Just across the Andon about twenty yards away was the railroad. Suddenly a lively scrap in which a handful of men on either side were involved was kicked up. A machine gun knocked up the ballast at the feet of the Yanks, one of whom was Evans. Victory was our boys' portion, and a German, wounded as he ran from the depot in which they were fortified, was probably shot by my buddy.

The machine gunners were captured by an engineer, he having walked in on them from the rear unawares. A little later, as I was sitting complacently on the bank of the murmuring stream, seven or eight Boche broke from the thicket within ten yards of me. Alarmed, I grabbed my gun but by that time saw they were unarmed. Behind them came their captor, the lone Yank engineer.

As night drew on, we crossed the creek and railroad, and the chow detail brought us some supper. Seeing Evans' wounded German beckoning to us, I reported it and a patrol was sent but did not bring him away as he doubtless desired. Far into the night his hideous cries resounded, but in the morning he was gone. His comrades had taken him away.

After dark we advanced to the foot of a hill in front of us and commenced to dig in but were ordered back on a line with the cemetery and the train road, and my platoon dug in on the railroad dump, which was only a yard high here. I did not envy one company, L, I believe, which had to dig in under the cemetery wall.

I am a Protestant of the deepest dye, but it did me good to look at the crucifix in the midst of the burial ground that afternoon. However, I could not think but how great a travesty on religion this war was. Here we Americans were fighting Germans to liberate the French people, and all three nationalities worshipped the same Christ, but there were murderous shells shrieking within a few feet of the image of the Prince of Peace and his followers had hurled the missiles and more embattled followers were cringing from the shells under the walls of the cemetery over which his benign image kept guard.

While Prather kept guard for the platoon I slipped away and filled our canteens with the water of the brook. It was not very sanitary but was wet and far better than none, which latter amount we had had all day and consequently were very dry.

We had taken Romagne that day and in doing so had broken the Kriemhilde Stellung, the famous third line that they thought could not be taken.[2] And furthermore the break was in its very center, while the divisions on either side of us failed to break through that day. But it was costly. Four of our company were dead, one of them being my platoon sergeant, Flynn, and my dear friend Shirey was mortally wounded, though I was ignorant of what had happened to him at the time. Also among the dead was a popular little Italian, Cupust by name. Our commander, First Lieutenant Pelton, had his leg broken with a piece of shell; Second Lieutenant Steele had a bullet pass through his liver; and the company was now commanded by Second Lieutenant McKee, who, although a bullet had gone through his wrist, was still with us. Sergeant Horn was wounded in the groin by a bullet, and my corporal, Steen, though slightly wounded, came back to us that night. Of my squad, six in number that morning, three had been hit, Armstrong being the worst wounded. Rake, although he had been knocked flat by a bullet that went through his helmet and mess kit, had only a grazed skin and a knot on the side of his head to show for it.

At last I had been through a battle and boyhood dreams of things military had come true. Men had been killed all around me, close about me, and many others wounded. Bullets had whizzed galore around me, one of them within six inches, and I had felt the thrill of shooting bullets at the enemy. I had been over the top!

Yet I was still all together and unwounded and a Yank from Mississippi dreamed of home down by the railroad beyond a captured town while sounds of buzzing trucks down the valley of the Andon proved that the Germans were moving what they could of their supplies.

11

Romagne

All America has a tragic interest in Romagne. On its outskirts is the Field of Honor where the dead collected from all the Meuse-Argonne battlefield are buried, these numbering some fifteen thousand. Several thousand of these have been brought back to American cemeteries, but for thousands of brokenhearted and weeping American parents and other relatives of the slain, Romagne will be the Mecca for years to come.[1] Romagne was the focal center of the Meuse-Argonne battle, which fact accounts for its being chosen as the place of burial of the American dead. It will thus be seen that our venture on the morning of the fourteenth of October was no unimportant affair, as it resulted in the break of the Kriemhilde Stellung, or German third line, at its midpoint.

The battlefield as a whole has been described as low on the east (the valley of the Meuse); low on the west (the valley of the Aire), with a broad ridge in the center called by some the whaleback.[2] This was not a plateau but a ridge intersected by numerous small valleys. The heights about Romagne are parts of this ridge. Romagne is a typical French village of about six hundred or seven hundred population, that is, it was before the war. It is in the deep narrow valley of the Andon River, which could be more properly called a brook. Its site in the valley is just a little ways after the depression turns to the east and becomes a transverse valley. So it is about as entirely surrounded by high hills as a place could well be.

In just what direction the Field of Honor is from Romagne I have never been able to determine. I had an intimate connection with the hills south of the town and the lower ridges both to the east and the west of it, so I must have seen the site of the American cemetery, though of course it was not there at that time and numbers to be

afterward interred therein were lying dead over the face of the landscape, and many who would occupy graves therein still had their life
blood surging through hearts athrob with patriotism and a desire to
fight the Boche.

So I awoke at dawn of the fifteenth beside the railroad tracks just
a little east of the town. The first thing that morning was a bit of
merry shooting at a German who came over the hill in front of us as
the target. He skedaddled back over the hill apparently unharmed,
although many rifles popped at him. The morning was foggy, and
there were not lacking those who cautioned that it might be an
American, but it wasn't.

Then we lined up to advance, I being eager to go, although with
no little apprehension. What was left of a platoon of twenty-four
hours ago now marched as two squads, a fact that was almost sickening as it was tragic to see my comrades melt away that way. Imagine
our chagrin when instead of winning new victories as we could have
done we halted on top of the hill only two hundred yards from the
starting point. I found a convenient shell hole and as Prather had
gone with the other squad spent a lonesome day reading my Testament nearly all day, which was singularly quiet in our sector, though
occasional bullets whizzed harmlessly over our heads.

I remember visiting a large dugout in the bank of the railroad cut
just below us that afternoon. As I look back this now seems to me to
have been dangerous as I was not at all sure of its being free of the
enemy. At one of the doors I stumbled over a burlap sack full of
what I at first thought to be bricks, but which proved to be loaves
of German bread that, it has been reported, was made partly out of
buds and bark of trees. I was hungry and sampled it, gouging out the
center of a loaf, in fact sampled it until it almost made me sick.

And this makes me think that I omitted to remark in my account
of the fourth and fifth of October that on each of those days my
comrades and I drank a small quantity of beer we had captured from
the Germans. Folks at home were afraid to drink out of their own
wells for fear of poison administered by the enemy, here we drank
beer that the enemy had left behind in their flight. It was the first
beer I had ever drunk. I tell folks sometimes that I drank it to see
how it tasted and to see if it were poisoned. The bread also had a
dual attraction for me. I wanted to see how it tasted and to allay the
pangs of hunger.

With night a slow drizzling rain set in. Try as I might my shelter half would not protect me, and my home was soon caving in and becoming a mass of mud. With visions of a horrible night in the mud and rain, worse happened—I was put on guard. Coffee, a little fellow from West Virginia, was my partner. We spent a miserable hour standing in the mud with the raindrops pattering on our helmets and slickers, while it seemed as if a very, very small squirrel was frisking around my vaccination scar.

Guard duty over, we decided to seek shelter from the rain. Repairing to the dugout, we found that it was occupied by the lieutenant and his staff. Seems as if it were almost full, for Evans, one of the runners, hearing my voice, insisted that I come down and sleep on the steps if I could not find a better place, but I preferred the night and rain and German shells to staying in a dugout with a lieutenant.[3]

There was just across the railroad a long, low frame building. It had been hit and splintered by a shell or two. Thither we repaired, and finding a room not badly injured we improvised a bed on a German wire cot. Hardly had we got set for a sleep when we heard voices. Two men came into the room and gruffly demanded what we were doing there. I recognized them as corporals and thinks I, "They have come to make us go back up on the hill but will have a funny time doing it, for even if we are punished for insubordination they can hardly think of a worse punishment than putting us out in the rain and mud and cold." Knowing they did not recognize us, I replied as harshly as they talked. The expected command to return to the hill did not come, and the corporals soon receded from their harsh attitude, and I discovered that instead of taking us back to the hill they had come to share our room with us and soon we were on pleasant terms. I remember that some fine particles of rain sifted through a broken-out window and down on me, but the shelter half over our blankets kept us from getting wet and we had a good night's rest even though some shells fell around the cabin.

October 16

With the first streaks of day the corporals, with advice to get back up on the hill before we were missed, left us. Coffee and I were in no rush to go, for business was not very lively as yet and this was the front line the same as on the hill, so we went when we got ready.

Then time began to hang heavily on my hands. I watched Allied airplanes above the hill to the southeast searching for our front line and finding it. I think the 125th was holding that hill. I watched a small barrage on a dugout in a stone pit across the way. It was a small German gun that was trained upon it and more than a dozen shells rained about it. I wondered why the Boche was so anxious about hitting a stone pit, but a comrade had run across a pair of rather poor field glasses; with their aid I discovered the entrance to the dugout. Evidently it was the enemy's intention to blockade the mouth of this and entrap the Yanks therein. An American machine gun cleverly camouflaged in a building near the stone pit had been talking in no uncertain terms to Fritz. If they did not discover its location they were not so discerning as I.

Things became monotonous, and I set out on an exploring trip, taking pains of course to go back of our lines. About seventy-five yards back of us was the railway station, which had almost escaped my attention up to that time. Thither I turned my steps. It was a trim little building, very substantial, and bordered so as to be very beautiful. As it was new and the railroad new, I imagined the Germans had built them since the war began. Very little damage had been done to the building save by machine-gun bullets, but slivered glass and bullet marks on the walls gave abundant evidence of their having come into contact with it. I walked around admiring the precision of the lines of the structure. Outside the waiting room door I turned and glanced up; there above the door was the word "Romagne." Till then I had not had the slightest idea of the name of the village we had taken.

The slow mist so characteristic of France kept up the greater part of the day. When it rained, the war spirit lagged and there was a great lull in the fighting. Only occasionally a resounding boom echoing over the landscape recalled our attention to the serious business in hand. The rain and the mud and the good roof of the depot induced me to decide to spend most of the day there. I was certainly as much benefit to the army there as I would have been out in the rain and was taking better care of one of Uncle Sam's soldiers. It is true that I was very cold as I could have no fire. I was hungry, too, and could find nothing edible at the depot save dried carrots, which were not very palatable.

The reader may wonder at the laxness of the discipline while here. All our commissioned officers had been wounded; First Lieutenant Pelton, the company commander, in the leg; Second Lieutenant Steele had been shot through the liver; and Second Lieutenant McKee had had a bullet through his wrist but stayed with us until the major ordered him back for treatment. We had only two sergeants left and very few corporals. It is true the major sent us a new lieutenant, but that worthy stayed in the dugout the two days he was with us—a very sensible act, too—and I never saw him. So the company stayed intact by pure Americanism and patriotism. Indeed, no matter how many officers we had had we could not have kept the position any better and probably would not have had any more men there. The few days letup in discipline was good on our morale and gave evidence of the stamina of the American army and the purposes for which we went overseas.

A chow detail came up about noon. I was watching the happenings and was there on the spot when dinner was served. My portion was a small loaf of bread and a can of salmon, the latter of which almost disappeared at one meal. The sun shone out for a few minutes while we were eating, a rather unusual occurrence, and a big shell fell across the creek at the foot of the hill and a score of places began smoking all around where it exploded. While I was wondering what it meant, I heard Steen, who was near me, saying, "What the hell." I asked him what it was and he replied, "Liquid fire."[4]

In my walking about that afternoon I came up to a man standing in the doorway of a dugout between my shell hole and the depot. The dugout had been literally full of men the night before, but the fellow informed me that orders had been issued to permit none except himself to stay there that night and that he could stay only because he had a bad cold. It seems that this cold did not prevent him from wanting to eat as he asked me for part of my loaf of bread. I gave him a large share on condition that he let me share his dugout that night. He traded readily.

When night came good old Joe Dennis from Arkansas and I sought the dugout. The fellow with whom I traded was absent but soon returned with a companion. As there was hardly room for four at the bottom of the place, we soon got into an unfriendly scramble and argument about it, which eventually became a quarrel. They were going to make us get out, but by dint of words and hobnails we held our place. A guard came by and inquired if anybody was down in the dugout who was not supposed to be. Our amiable friends immediately reported Dennis and me, who received harsh orders to get out. We made the guard believe we were coming out, but ten minutes later when we had made no move the other fellows asked if we were going and received the answer, "Hell, no." Along came the corporal of the guard and gave us identical orders to move, again we promised, and sat steady in the dugout. After a while as we were getting sleepy another guard came along, but his success in extracting two Yanks was not very evident. Then the sergeant of the guard ordered us out, we promising to go with no intention to go. Another corporal waked us up and we broke our promise to him as also to another sergeant later in the night. Two privates, two guards, two corporals, and two sergeants tried to get us out of the dugout and each failed, for Dennis and I were there when daylight came. Such a pal was Dennis! I do not wish for a better and would like to tell him how much I appreciate even yet his valiant stand with me that night, but I'll never be able to do so in this world for he was killed far east of the Meuse the last week of the war, as was also my bedfellow of the night before.

October 17

This was a day almost devoid of interest if I except a visit to Romagne in the afternoon. I spent the day on the line and at the depot. The battle somehow was at an ebb in our sector, due perhaps to our holding the eastern side of the salient near its base. I have always thought we could have taken a town about two miles in our front and wanted to (a little), but they say it was not in our sector. Many times while here I walked down the skyline of our hill surely in sight of the Germans but was never hit, nor did I fear being hit, although bullets whistled by occasionally. Guess I was getting callous to battle and careless with my life, for it was risky.

I took some canteens and with a few companions went back to Romagne a half kilometer for water. This we found in abundance at the town pump.

Hearing music, we sought it and found a YMCA man playing a piano for some officers in an erstwhile German *Soldatenheim* or soldier's home. We listened for a while and then went into the nearby church, which had been hit by three or four shells and was in ruins, the daylight glaring through walls and ceiling in a curious way.

Shells falling in the town caused us to exit hastily.

12

Relief

Those periodical shellings of the town of Romagne went on all the time I was beyond the place. It has been claimed that the shells were German and from across the Meuse, but it appeared to me that they were coming from the southwest and I always will believe that they were American shells falling short. Strange that the gunners were missing their calculations so far, but I don't see any reason to try to plaster the matter over and say it was something it was not. Whatever the origin, we felt safer in the open country.

On the way back to the line, a comrade offered me a taste of what he said was German honey. It was sweet but not very delicious to my way of thinking; still it was more experience.

During the day I had decided that I was going to spend the night (which did not give evidence of being rainy as the sun shone some in the afternoon) in the basement of the depot where were already some bed sacks once used by Germans. Best of all the place was surrounded by concrete walls, which would be some protection against shells, but my plans went awry, as did those of the three comrades I invited to go with me. Just here I will say that in another part of the basement American soldiers stayed all the while I was in that sector.

This hill just beyond the depot marks the flood tide of the Red Arrow in its first tour of duty in the Meuse-Argonne.[1] At twilight a welcome relief came and we backtracked through the ruined village and took position on a sloping hillside nearly two kilometers back of the front line. Not having any buddy I allowed myself to be adopted by two kind Pennsylvanians, Davis and Lehman. After a tour of guard duty we spent a fairly restful night in a small place where we had dug in.

October 18

Before I forget it will say we had been relieved by F Company of our own regiment and that my two new buddies lived near Wilkes-Barre, Pennsylvania. Lehman was a devout Catholic, while Davis didn't profess any particular religion. I knew them for some time; in fact. Davis and I parted company at Camp Mills.[2]

It was on this hillside that I had probably the most harrowing experiences of my war career. A German gun had a peculiar way of shelling us. We could hear a shell drop and explode we judged approximately four hundred yards in front of us; a few seconds later another would fall about three hundred yards from us in a direct line with the first; a wait of a few more seconds and one would fall another hundred yards closer; another very short interval and one would land on the hill almost exactly one hundred yards in front of us. Of course our fears would be growing all the while, and now we would be looking for the next one to come another one hundred yards farther and fall plump in the foxhole with us. So with bated breath, taut nerves, and hearts thumping loudly against our ribs we would await our death, wondering how badly we would be scattered over the landscape, and three poor mortals would cringe and writhe in an almost death agony while the seconds ticked away and seemed minutes, then would come the hellish messenger of death with a shriek and a rush and a roar while we cringed the more—sure that death had now come when, wonderful to relate and joyful, the shell would scream over us and fall a full two hundred yards beyond. Not once did this happen but at least a dozen times in the two days we were there. And what made it more distressing for me was the fact that my heart pained me severely whenever excited due to the shell having fallen so close to me. A few nights before, we had all of death but the dying.

Needless to say that when a shell passed we thanked God for sparing our lives and lay limp and inert for quite a while after it passed. Just why the German gunner should have adjusted his range that way I cannot tell you unless it was the hand of Providence, which I am firmly persuaded was the case.

Perhaps the reader will wonder why our fears subsided when a shell passed over us. Well, we had learned that a German gunner never depressed his gun; he always raised it, and so shot farther every time. If he wanted to shoot back toward him he brought it back to the first range and began all over again. This was true every time I noticed it, and this one particular gunner was exact in his ways. Then, too, you will likely ask why we didn't move and go to a safer place. Some other place might have been as dangerous and this was our station, and as discipline was a little better now we could not leave.

I mentioned that we had a new lieutenant who stayed in his dugout and never gave me a sight of him. Will say that he was nice to us, sending back and purchasing a lot of things from the YMCA and giving them to us, for which he has my thanks. Soon he was transferred to another command and our one remaining sergeant became company commander. The next day he was ordered back and sent to the officers' training school. Similar orders came the next day to Corporal Ogden, who succeeded him, and the command of the company fell to Corporal McDonald.

Midafternoon of the eighteenth found me asking McDonald permission to go across the valley to the scene of our battle on the fourteenth to salvage a blanket. This was granted, and I set out with the idea of securing my pack that in my hurry when we went through Romagne I had forgotten. This I found to have been rifled but managed to find a good blanket nearby. Also I picked up a splendid Springfield rifle. In spite of four days in the rain it was in good condition. I had a supply of ammunition in my belt and an AEFer can guess what was going to happen to the Chauchat. What distressed me most was the fact that our dead were still lying as they had fallen on the fourteenth though seven men from other outfits had been grouped together near the foot of the hill.

So my Pennsylvania buddies and I were warmer that night by one blanket.

October 19

The nineteenth passed almost uneventfully except that that harrowing experience of the shells was repeated several times during the day.

Will say that one reason I suffered so from the cold on the front was that I still had on my summer underclothes and the top one could have been warmer. Too, since the early days of the drive, I had been suffering from dysentery. This and lack of food caused me to be very weak. My rheumatism and the pain in my heart when excited were excruciating. So, I guess I did my part of suffering, and I know I stayed when many less afflicted went to the hospital.[3]

During the day my buddies and I fixed us a "jake" place in a deep shell hole near our old quarters and were already in bed, although it was just after dark, when a small commotion called us out. Glory be, relief had come at last.[4]

Late in the afternoon we had drawn a new lieutenant, King by name, and there had been other signs of relief, but we had almost ceased to expect anybody to come and take our place. An element of the brave Eighty-ninth Division had come to take our place, and we welcomed them heartily. Brave fellows, they were now to go through the mill![5]

Eighty-four men of the 246 men and three officers we had started with from Chatonrupt a month before rolled packs and marched away toward Cierges, although we soon turned to the right and took the hill road that led back to the Harness Lodge Woods. Thin clouds scudded over a sallow moon that occasionally gave a little peep down on the marching men. We were not alone on the road that night but met many other elements of the Eighty-ninth going to take the places of other Thirty-second Division men. Some of my comrades insisted on telling them what a place they were going into, but I finally prevailed on some of my buddies not to discourage them.

The road was hard and dry as flint and our hobnails clicked merrily on it. Never had my pack seemed so light, as indeed it seldom was as I had only a makeshift now, never did my feet lend themselves so willingly to a hike.[6] Glory be! After a tour of duty of nearly three weeks I was going to the rear. After facing death in a thousand hideous forms, my life was spared for a season. Many of my comrades had been slain, but my life had been miraculously spared. So with thankful heart and cheered body I tramped along. "Joy is the best of wine" and my cup was running over.

As I said, we had spent nearly three weeks in the lines. Three divisions had fought on either side of us in that time and the casualties of the Red Arrows numbered nearly six thousand.[7] Now, our duty done, and well done, we were leaving our positions in the hands of worthy successors and were headed for a well-earned rest.

I didn't care how far we went that night, the farther the better— in fact I wanted to get clear of all danger of falling shells—but the familiar woods southwest or more nearly west of Cierges loomed ahead of us, and we entered them by the road we had left and sought again a home in the vicinity of the Harness Lodge.

Davis happened not to belong to the same platoon that Lehman and I did and, having to go with his part of the company, the little Catholic and I were left to buddy together. Other troops had camped there since we had left, and my pal and I found a foxhole some of them had dug and made our bed there for the night. This place was not very ample and though it was long enough it lacked some in width, as when one of us lay on his back the other had to lie on his side, and when one had to change position he invariably woke the other.

Hardly had we got to bed when the moonlight faded out, the moon hiding herself behind thick clouds, and a slow misty rain began. This did not trouble us as our shelter half caught the rain, and as soon as the interstices in the cloth were filled with water we experienced a feeling of warmth and sank into a sweet slumber. But there was a gun about two hundred yards back of us—one of our heavy artillery guns—that every once in a while sent a message over to Fritz. Whenever it fired it waked me, and so my night's rest though cozy was a series of catnaps.

Sunday, October 20

No more dismal Sunday could have dawned. The rain, it seemed, had steadily been getting harder, until now it seemed that a regular marching rain was falling, by that I mean the kind that usually happened along when we marched anywhere. But I did not mind it, for the danger was some less and soon we were marching to the rear. This time when we came to the edge of the woods we turned to the right and kept on through the rain and the slush.

My little friend, Lehman, was surely a devoted Catholic, for he prayed constantly no matter where he was and always aloud. The fellow who did more praying on the front than I must have been an expert, but I did mine privately. Not so with Lehman, and he would call anyone's hand if he should say or do anything he ought not to. Lehman was a good fellow, but his constant praying finally got on my nerves, and soon after we started on our hike he let in for the 'steenth time that morning. We were marching along through slush shoe-mouth deep and the company and others were along, but he began his prayers again out big and loud and it rasped my nerves harshly, so I proceeded to bawl him out and tell him I preferred his devotions to be private.

I did wrong, I know, but Lehman returned not a word. His public orisons ceased, but I noticed his lips moving frequently in silent prayer. About two miles down the road, I got sorry for having treated the boy so and apologized. His reply was a just rebuke and made me sorrier still. He said: "Baker, I can only pray for those who mistreat me." I think of this little incident often and sometimes laugh over it and sometimes I do not. In spite of it, Lehman and I became pretty good buddies.

The road turned and twisted and the rain fell steadily; the slush became deeper and deeper; the murky clouds shut out all airplane spying upon us; the guns were somewhat silent on the front; and the battle-scarred remnant of the once proud 128th, looking more like a small battalion than a regiment, wound down the road to the rear, twisting and turning as the road turned much like a tawny caterpillar.

Once at a wayside kitchen I got a handful of the best cooked rice, but our officers would not halt to let us get more so I ate it as I walked and the memory lingers yet. Fifteen kilometers on the road brought us to a dripping woodland. Here we rested on a dreary stretch of road. A few minutes later we had orders to leave the road and build fires in the woods. This was not an unwelcome order, though I was almost at a loss to see how we could build a fire with so much water on the landscape. But they were soon going and felt so pleasant that I was glad of the halt, for I was beginning to feel fatigued very much. I had been noticing the German signs, and I think the one that applied to those woods read "Cheppywald." Somehow or other the impression was left on me that we were going to stay here only an hour or so, but the gray day darkened to night and we were still there, indeed night was not far off when we stopped about three o'clock. I was eager to resume the march, for I had conjured up visions of pleasant billets in some French village, but we did not start and soon it was apparent that we would pass the night there. We stayed thirteen days.

Company K, 128th Infantry, Thirty-second Division, in support near Juvigny, August 29, 1918. SOURCE: 111-SIGNAL CORPS 21908.

General William G. Haan conversing with a German lieutenant, October 9, 1918. SOURCE: 111-SIGNAL CORPS 26679.

Prisoner aged perhaps fifteen captured near Montfaucon, October 15, 1918. SOURCE: 111-SIGNAL CORPS 26682.

Near Romagne, October 18, 1918. SOURCE: 111-SIGNAL CORPS 26697.

Inspection of 128th Infantry by General John J. Pershing near Disdorf, Germany, December 22, 1918. SOURCE: 111-SIGNAL CORPS 44442.

13

Cheppywald

The dreary twentieth darkened quietly to night, and the slow drizzle besprinkled a bivouac in the woods. As the sky was overcast, airplanes could not annoy us and the fires kept going all night. Lehman and I erected our pup tent, but as he had only two blankets and I the meager sum of one, we did not sleep very warm, and several times during the night I went to the fire and sat in the rain by it trying to thaw out. There was not enough rain to hamper the campfires but enough to wet one if he stayed in it.

The next morning dawned almost as dreary as the preceding one except that there was not so much rain falling. Confident that we would soon pull out on the resumed march to the rear, I arose in good spirits, but the morning dragged on and we still sat by the fireside, but even this was much better than we had been experiencing.

I don't remember whether it was on Monday or Tuesday that the noncoms were summoned to go away to hear the general speak, but I do know that when they returned we prodded them with questions and were comforted (?) by the news that General Haan had assured them that there would be no rest for the Thirty-second Division until the war had ended and that these woods were all the pleasant billets we would know during our rest spell.

So we settled down to the dull routine of camp life. This was not so bad, for I will say here that a war is not so bad if there is only fighting and resting between times to do, but for a soldier to be put to useless menial tasks between times lessens one's morale and increases his disgust of service in the army more than anything that can happen. That being true, I have no very disagreeable memories of Cheppywald, for our time was largely spent around the campfires and what time we were not there we were engaged in useful work. It is true we did some manual of arms, but my new corporal gave his squad more "Rest" than any other orders. One day I spent on KP—volunteering to do it—and one on guard. You may rest assured that when I was on KP, I had a full day's rations. The day's guard duty was not arduous, in fact it has left so little impression on my memory that I can barely remember where my post was, although I remember that my special order was to keep the boys from rolling a car along a narrow-gauge tram road.

The reader will please not get it into his head that we were out of danger, for a swish very like a falling tree followed by an explosion over and anon resounded from the foot of the hill about a half kilometer away, nor did we know how soon the range would be raised and the missiles fall in our midst. And, too, the second night our fires burned brightly as if we were miles away from the enemy, although the rain had ceased and if I remember rightly it cleared off in the night. Just after dark of the third night a multitude of fires were twinkling through the forest, when suddenly a whir of an airplane was heard and then "Bang! bang! bang!" went three bombs dropped from it. Immediately the cry "Fires out!" rang through the woods repeated and rerepeated, and in less time than it takes to tell it the woods were in inky blackness. We heard that three men were killed by the bombs over in the 126th Infantry, but whether this was true or not I cannot say.

The company was reorganized in Cheppywald. It was almost sickening to note that although there were at least four squads of men larger than I when we went into the lines, now I was one of the largest members of the company. What was left of the first half of my platoon became a squad, that is, three squads had dwindled to one. The company had dwindled from four large platoons to two small ones. I remember how we lined up on the little railroad through the forest and the man next to my left who never came back. I remember, too, the day when the sergeant picked out Banholzer of my squad for a stretcher bearer and then called for a volunteer to go with him. None had responded, and the sergeant fixing his eyes on me asked if I didn't want to. I was saying "Yes" and another man spoke out and said he would be one, so I was relieved of the duty.

Our corporal was Konkle from Michigan—the erstwhile private who had drilled us in the woods of Lavoye. Steen was given a two weeks' furlough and went back to the south of France. He had given me a revolver to carry as automatic rifleman and I mistakenly thought it was his property and took better care of it than I would otherwise. Will say in regard to our new corporal, that in my opinion there were few better ones in the army.

My little Catholic pal and I got along very well, except when he asked me if my Bible told about Jesus. I couldn't help but bawl him out then but when he apologized so abjectedly I got sorry for him and freely forgave him for what I had said to him. Perhaps anyway my questions about the Catholics and their ways of doing were quite as silly.

But Lehman developed trench feet and I did to some extent. The poor fellow spent all his waking moments at night in prayer, and the burden of them was that the war might end and he get home by Christmas. Several nights whenever I moved the cover the least bit it would awaken him. I couldn't lie still all the time, and when I turned over the cover would hurt his feet and his piteous pleas and quarreling words about it have alternately made me sorry for him and aggravated at him. I know the pain must have been intense. Finally he went to the hospital and my farewell to him was perhaps forever, for he never returned to the old outfit.

Lehman's leaving left me with one blanket and half of a tent, but those stalwart West Virginians, Prather and Rake, invited me to stay with them, which I did for one night, and when a new man was added to the squad in the person of Barrett of Tennessee, who had returned from the hospital, I formed a co-partnership with him for the remainder of our stay in Cheppywald. And one day, in addition to the men returned from the hospital, we were overjoyed to welcome thirty-nine new men and a new lieutenant. The new men had come from the old Thirty-ninth Division, and I began to wonder if Willie Depriest, whom I had left at Massay, was among the new replacements to other companies.

Thus passed a week slowly but surely, with the guns booming all day long every day in a wide semicircle to the north of us and the occasional swish of a shell over the hill from us. If we had had plenty to eat here our stay would have been pleasant.

October 27

The fourth Sunday of October dawned bright and clear, at least I remember the beautiful sunshine, though it seems as if there were some clouds during the day. It was announced that there would be preaching at 10:00 or 11:00 o'clock, I have forgotten which, and that the place was by the First Battalion headquarters. I got up a bunch of four or five fellows, one of whom was a Catholic we called Frenchy from the fact that he was a Louisiana Frenchman. Setting out for the place of worship nearly an hour before time appointed, we began to ask of nearly everyone we met the location of the First Battalion P.C.[1] Always it was a little farther and a little farther until we came to a water tank, erected by the Germans no doubt, and certainly used by them. We quenched our thirst and were then directed to a path leading over a hill to the east. Some other inquiries brought us to an excavated place on the north side of the hill and quite in the woods. Frenchy had insisted that services were to be down at our kitchen and I found out later that Catholic services were held there that day, and so I had taken a Catholic from his church service and carried him to a Protestant service.

A very few minutes elapsed after we arrived before some several other men came, and then some officers, the band, and a chaplain appeared on the hillside above the excavation. Where the chaplain stood was a little level spot. Down in the flat of the excavation were mostly enlisted men; there were present in all, the few pieces of the band, officers and all, about forty men.

An old-time hymn was announced and was led by the band. I'm sure most of the men present knew most of it by memory, but the singing was scanty, the officers doing most of it. I did not sing for one time in life; I sat on a large stone with my companions around me and almost had to look over my shoulder to see the band, and although I wanted to sing, my heart was too full for song. It was the regular Protestant service. The chaplain, a slender man of medium height, prayed a fervent prayer that went to the hearts and as he prayed for the folks at home carried us in spirit far across the Atlantic.

And then the sermon. I suspect I shall never hear the like again. To say the talk was splendid will be to put it mildly indeed. The sun was shining through the somber October woods, the breeze tilting and waving gently the leaves still in the boughs, while far to the north on the wide semicircle the guns boomed an accompaniment, and once or twice the swish of shells falling over the hill lent a touch of solemnity and provided a setting that one will have to search far to find. The thrilling words of the preacher lifted me up, up and brought solace to my bleeding heart. The martial sounds and the nearer solitude of the forest must have attuned his utterances and lent fire to his speech.

And after the last song and benediction we shook hands with the preacher, he giving a word of comfort and cheer whenever he thought proper, but I wrung his hand in silence for my heart was too full for utterance. I never learned the preacher's name or denomination, though I wish I had. I heard some weeks later that one of our chaplains was killed while burying the dead but hope it was a mistake and that this gifted preacher is still healing the wounds of the heart and soul. If he reads this, I hope he will write me.

After services we returned the mile and a half to our bivouac, refreshed and renewed in spirit and really feeling like we had been to church. At the service it was announced that Bishop Hughes of the Northern Methodist Church would preach that afternoon down on the valley road.[2] Had I known that it was perhaps scarcely a half mile from our bivouac, I am sure I would have gone. As it was we idled around the campfire all afternoon, I chancing to get hold of a recent issue of the Paris edition of the *Chicago Tribune*, which served me for a Sunday paper.

October 28

First on the program next morning was a trip to the delousing station. We went back three or four miles to what had been the town of Avocourt. You remember, I told you of passing through it just before dawn in the thick darkness late in September. It was the worst mutilated town I saw while over there, scarcely a wall was more than waist high, and the American engineers were using the place as a quarry, taking thence the stones to use in repairing the roads.

Don't ask me how long it had been since we had taken a bath—bathtubs and showers were not plentiful in the Argonne, and the weather was too cold for swimming, and the gunfire of the enemy too hot for canary baths. The shower baths at the delousing plant were splendid considering everything, the handout of new heavy woolen underwear most welcome, and the heating our outer garments were subjected to effectually rid them of any chance inhabitants of the order Cootie Americanus, of which only one had bothered me, and he probably finding life alone not good for him had departed.[3] It took the company some time to go through the plant and as each got ready to go back to camp he repaired out to the side of the road nearby but back a little north on same.

While standing there idly watching what was in sight and gloating silently over my new cleanly condition, a company of Yanks swung down the road from the north. Remembering that a new detachment had come from the Thirty-ninth, I scanned their faces as they passed us thinking I might see Willie Depriest, whom I had left at Massay. I didn't see him, but there was a familiar face among them. Recovering sufficiently from my shock to hail him, I gave him a shock in turn. It was my cousin—the soldier who lived closest to me in old Mississippi—Carlos Dean. Neither of us knew the other was in France, though we had fought through a great battle near each other—we had parted at Camp Pike.

He halted a little ways down the road, and I went down to greet him and speak a few words but did not get to talk long as M Company had orders to fall in. I had learned though that he was in M Company of the 127th Infantry and bivouacking near us in the same woods, and determined to visit him.

October 29–31

Off and on we had been working on a diminutive rifle range, which consisted of two layers of logs cut nearby with a six-foot layer of earth between them. It was some eight feet high and fourteen or sixteen long. I labored quite a bit on this but did not mind it. Finishing it on the twenty-ninth, the new third platoon was put immediately to trying it out. I somehow wanted to shoot some myself, but only the third platoon ever used the rifle range while we were there.

I have no clear recollection of anything worth telling about happening on the morning of the thirtieth, but in the afternoon we had a battalion maneuver over a broad hilltop sparsely timbered but covered with a thick growth of bushes and queer weeds. We took position in an old German trench and stayed there an hour or so, likely for the benefit of some new officers. An elderly French soldier, happening along on our maneuver, observed us a bit and then laughingly said, "Beaucoup rabbits," that is, "Lots of rabbits." Whether we gave him the idea of hunting rabbits merely or he was meaning that we would have plenty of Germans to hunt as rabbits, I had no means of knowing.

On the thirty-first we went out for a division maneuver to a hill a mile to the north of us. I was dreading it as someone had narrated the news that it was to be an all-day affair and that we would come back dreadfully fatigued. While waiting for the maneuver to begin we took morning exercises and were in the midst of a big game of "whip to the right" when a sergeant came to me and told me I had orders to report to band headquarters.

With some misgivings I set out, inquiring the way as I went, and ran across some men belonging to my friend Dean's company, from whom I learned the exact location of that company's camp. After an hour or two I found the band. It was on a gentle declivity under the trees through whose leafless boughs the sun was glinting. I approached the sergeant, whose name was Needles, I think, and asked what was wanted of me. He informed me that my application for a place in the band had been disapproved because I had not put my company and regiment on my application. I had not thought of turning in my name as an applicant and I know the neglect referred to was a woeful mistake, as I took pains to make my outfit clearly distinguishable, in fact that was all I remember putting on the paper besides my name. I held my tongue, however, as I really didn't want to get into the band no way and listened to the sergeant as he cheerily informed me that the war would soon be over and that there would be no time to train a new beginner before the parades began. So with better courage I turned my steps back to the maneuver grounds.[4] The company was gone, where I did not know, and not a Yank was in sight. So I went back to camp and spent a solitary and pleasant day by the campfire. Late in the afternoon the other boys returned dog-tired.

After supper, Short gave Evans and me permission to go over to see Dean in M Company, 127th. I was anxious to visit him that night

as the presentiment had been growing on me that a new trip to the
lines was close at hand and I wanted to see my friend while I could.

It was a comparatively easy matter to find M Company, 127th,
but not so easy to find Dean, but finally we located him down at the
bottom of a small stone pit with a very small cavity in its walls for a
home. His two or three comrades welcomed us also and joined
heartily in the talk for a time, but one by one they left us and retired
and the three of us Mississippi boys sat around the smoldering fire in
the Argonne.

From Dean we learned the results of the Mississippi elections in
August. He had heard from home a time or two, but we had never,
so in a way we established liaison with home again, and while the
night dragged on we hovered over the dying embers and talked of
past and present and future, of war and of peace, of sweethearts and
home but mostly of home.

14

The Last Drive

While we were talking with Dean, almost imperceptibly the cannonading on the front increased in intensity. It was with sinking heart that I sensed the beginning of a new drive that would mean the death of so many, many men, and would cause me to go through the hell of battle again and perhaps find a soldier's grave, yet withal it was to be the drive that brought peace and cleared France of her foes.

The more the embers of the little campfire smoldered the louder grew the cannonading and more livid the glow in the north, and finally when we bade Dean good night, for aught we knew for the last time, a perfect barrage was going on.

Evans and I walked home without much being said. On the hard, dry road near the bivouac we met a marching column—it was a regiment going toward the front, more proof of a new drive. Thinking that our own 126th would be leading the way into the fray as it had done before, I asked if the regiment were the 126th and was told that it was the Sixteenth Infantry of the First Division—our immortal First Division.[1]

And to bed with aching hearts, listening to the uproar on the semicircle to the north, mentally bidding farewell anew to home and loved ones, for I knew more fighting was in store.

Five o'clock came with the guns still booming, but louder than before. I lay and listened while first one and then another of my neighboring companies was called up to roll packs, and when the sepulchral order, "M Company, roll packs," came, I made quick work of packing up in the thick darkness.

And then dawned the first day of November. Cool and dry, with the sad sun wanly smiling over scenes of carnage, but, thank God, the drive begun that day was the last.

All day long we sat around our campfires listening ever for the order to move that did not come, listening to the horrid booming far to the north that was blended into one continuous roar, wishing to go to the fray, wishing to stay away in the same breath, talking the talk of camp and army, rereading the Paris daily now a week old, talking of home, talking of peace, until the roar died down about four o'clock and we knew a new victory or a defeat had come to American arms.

I remember a conversation that took place that day. It ran something like this:

I said, "Fellows, I don't want to go back to the lines again, for next week is going to be the last week of the war and I don't want to get killed that late in the game."

One of the fellows said, "Yes, if a man had been over here three years ago or even one and had got killed, it would have been a mercy for he would have been saved all this suffering, but now it's different."

Banholzer added, "You are right. I wouldn't mind having been killed away back then, but it would be terrible to get killed the last week of the war, and if I were to get knocked off the last day, why, I'd never get over it."

This raised a laugh of course. And now I will anticipate my story enough to say that by the irony of fate that brave soldier was instantly killed less than two hours before the guns became silent on Armistice Day and after he knew they would do so.[2]

And, having stayed "on the alert" all day, at nightfall we unrolled our packs and slept in our accustomed places.

November 2

Three a.m. found me listening to the other companies receiving their orders to roll packs, and when ours came I was ready to go shortly. This time there was no "on the alert," for we filed down to the bluff on the roadside and waited our turn of the marching order. War's grim business was again at hand, and verily for me the few days yet remaining were the most horrible of all the war days I ever experienced.

Of course, we did not know whether we were moving up in support of a victorious army or to take the place of a defeated or perhaps hard-pressed division. Soon we decided the latter was the fact, for we were marching in almost double quick time and I yet fail to see where there was any need of it. How we stood it I do not know, but there were few who fell out.

Dawn found us still toiling onward but at a slower pace. Back the same road we had come nearly two weeks before, back by the Harness Lodge Woods, in sight of Cierges, but we turned to the left and went through the ruined town of Gesnes, which will be remembered by many AEFers with unpleasantness.

In Gesnes, a K.C. man stood beside the line of march and gave each soldier as he passed two cigarettes.[3] Most of the boys did not like the taste of them, but we appreciated them and the spirit that gave them, even though I did not smoke.

It was almost a day's march when we reached Gesnes, though the lines did not seem to be much closer than when we had started. I thought perhaps we would camp in or around the village, but we swung into the road that leads to the north and kept on for four wearisome kilometers.

Everywhere the landscape was covered with the wreckage of war, though everything was quiet in this immediate vicinage and the country wildly beautiful with a gigantic hill frowning over the plain.

To this hill in our immediate front we marched and up it, tired as we were, almost to its very crest. The sun had kept itself behind the clouds nearly all day, and now well past the meridian peeped forth at intervals to cheer us with its light.

The high hill we were now on is north of Gesnes and west or northwest of Romagne. I have always thought it was the Côte Dame Marie so hardly fought over by our own 127th and also the Rainbow Division.[4] It was bad enough to climb the hill, let alone run the Germans off at the same time as some Yanks certainly had done. In the hollow beyond us was a battery of American heavy artillery.

I slept with Rake of W.Va. Poor fellow, I was tired and almost sick and quite irascible and grumbled at him about several trifles. He was a good scout or he would have knocked my block off, for there was no need of grumbling. Twilight and rain fell together, but we were comfortable in our hillside bed.

November 3

The day was spent quietly around the campfires near the hill's crest. Corporal Konkle went back to the hospital in the p.m. and we drew another not so good.

One of the things I shall remember was our good chaplain going through the woods halting with each platoon for a short prayer; though he was a Polish Roman Catholic the little exhortation and prayer joined in devoutly by many were in keeping with the situation and comforting to our sorely tried hearts. (Lest I forget it, will say his name was Mikolaicjak.) This prayer was intended to increase our morale, but it worked oppositely for we knew now we were headed for the front; it was proof sufficient.

At twilight we packed up and sat down to wait. I have a pleasant memory of that two hours' wait, for a bunch of boys a bit up the hill took a notion to sing and under the leadership of the irrepressible Lott, a singer of no mean ability, made the welkin ring. They sang practically all the songs the soldiers knew and some of them two or three times, nor did they forget to sing that classic of the army entitled "Home! Boys, Home!"

But the singing came to a close and the order to march caused an effect that struggled with the elevation of the singing.

A few raindrops were already falling when we marched single file around the precipitous hillside (in the valley several lights twinkled far below us), then over the crest and down through the darkness of the far slope.

At length we reached a road that seemed to me to run northwest, but the probabilities are that it ran east. The rain was now falling freely, but we went on, yes, on and on, the rain getting harder, the road getting sloppier, the soldiers sleepier and more fatigued. What little rest we got was while waiting for the troops in front of us to get out of our way. How I envied the boys in the pup tents beside the road. At that particular time it was my idea of rest, for I was tired and sleepy, wet to the skin, and when we stopped soon suffered with the cold. And the packs weighed far along toward a ton.

Once as we halted on the rain-soaked road an army Ford, evidently a courier car, sputt-sputtered down the road and stopped abreast of us. It was having a Ford fit, of course, and the occupants were angry. The boys as usual remembering the U.S.A. days were yelling, "Let me ride" as the car stopped.

"Come, get in and you can have it," said one of the occupants in an exasperated tone.

"No, thank you," returned an M Company sergeant, "I have all I can tote now."

And the company laughed regardless of sufferings.

The march was continued. We went through a village at almost double quick. The place looked familiar. It was Romagne. A building with bales of hay stored inside and well lighted looked like a good billet to me, but we left the town and went on.

Several kilometers farther an artilleryman on a high bank beside the road gave notice that a gun was going to shoot. Though expecting it, it excited and almost deafened me.

This gun and its mates on the hill above were firing toward the east and, of course, were aimed at the enemy across the Meuse, though it seemed strange that they should shoot eastward as we had been pressing northward so long.

Nearby was another ruined village with a conspicuous church with a weather vane in its center. Its houses were destroyed but, oh, so inviting! I had a notion to fall out deliberately, and some of the boys did. We had not far to march now as just beyond the town we stopped and between pushing and pulling got each other up a steep bank onto a field, level but filled with shell holes.

It was now about two in the morning. The rain had ceased, but the prospect of sleeping on the soaked field was not alluring. Nevertheless Banholzer and I fixed our bed and soon were asleep.

November 4

When daylight came we resumed the march, but it ended abruptly a quarter of a mile away in a pleasant woods.

I took the canteens and went to the town for water. It was the village of Cunel, remembered by the Fifth Division. The church was the most conspicuous feature of the town and was damaged somewhat. Someone told me that the Americans had to well nigh destroy it to dislodge the German watchers from its belfry. Already there was a YMCA establishment in the town.

November 5

I woke up sick. There wasn't much the matter with me; I just had a bad cold, was so hoarse I could not talk above a whisper, had a headache, dysentery, and a fever. A squad mate, Bonner by name, was also ailing but he had one less ailment than I. So as soon as possible we repaired to the doctor.

That worthy, a highly competent (?) authority, got us mixed up and sent Bonner to the hospital because he had a fever and I didn't. But he either didn't know when a fellow had a fever or lied, one of the two. He gave me a handful of medicine, and I went back and rolled up in my blankets and spent the day, most of the time viewing the phantasmagoria conjured up by my high fever. Still there was one pleasant feature of my day of pain. My buddy, Banholzer, was as good as a brother to me and I did not lack for tender care. The medicine helped me lots and I thought by morning I would be well.

I ate only a few bites for supper—didn't feel like eating and was preparing for a restful night—when at twilight came the killjoy order, "M Company, roll packs."

Several of the boys tried to get me not to attempt the hike, but I decided to go as far as I could. My head was light and at times I felt giddy and could hardly control my feet, but I stayed with it. We took the river road that runs from Cunel to Brieulles. The road had dried in a hurry and marching was not such a trial. How far we had advanced I do not know, but we were going down a slope at a fast pace when suddenly three shells fell just ahead of us beside the road. Did the Germans know we were coming and were they trying to halt us? It looked so.

Well, we halted, and as more shells fell, "to the reared," going back something like a mile and off onto another road, where we lay down on the roadside for some hours, I taking several naps. I have some distant memories of a couple of French 75s on a high bluff by the road; they almost scared me out of my wits a time or two.

November 6

About two o'clock we resumed the march, this time going silently down the slope and without shelling. Down in the valley of the Meuse, we passed the ruined town of Brieulles and then set out across the swampy plain of the river. We came to a diminutive stream and crossed it on a new pontoon bridge. Gosh, those engineers were brave to build this under fire! On farther we came to a broad expanse of water. It was the Meuse Canal, and here was the bulk of the water of the stream. It too was bridged with a new pontoon bridge. I could tell this in spite of the thick darkness. It was about an hour before day, so we crossed the Meuse in the face of the enemy between five and six o'clock.[5]

Silently we tiptoed across the canal bridge—another monument to indomitable engineers. At the farther end stood a guard. Halting within a few feet of the guard for a few moments we engaged him in conversation. I heard him say, "Yes, they have taken a few shots at me tonight; the bullets whizzed mighty close."

In an agonized voice someone asked, "How far is it to the front line?"

The reply was, "About one hundred fifty yards."

This conversation was carried on in an undertone. In reply to another question we learned that the Fifth Division boys had crossed the day before.[6]

Across the bridge we halted again. Slowly the dawn came. At the foot of a huge bluff about fifty yards from the river we discerned small olive drab mounds. What we saw were blankets covering American soldiers.

Then in the gray dawn we scaled the bluff where it ceased to be a bluff and became a hill. Taking position on the sloping hilltop we were once again in the front line.

Banholzer was elsewhere as a stretcher bearer, so I had no buddy now and felt strangely aloof from the company though it was all about me. I remember eating my breakfast of supper's remains while looking back over the landscape, which was singularly beautiful. Though I was sick when the night march was begun, I had stood it fine—a good example of what will power will do, and save for the feeling of being weak I was okay.

And before I tell you about going over the top at eight o'clock, will mention something of the military status at that time. The doughty Fifth Division had advanced on the first of November driving the Boches before them. The line at their particular sector was a peculiar one, and the sector continually widened fan-shaped. The entire American front was rapidly advancing and the Fifth Division found it trying to keep pressing on in a steadily widening sector, but they did it, putting in every infantry unit in their front line and then putting in the engineers. Finally, they borrowed a regiment from the Thirty-second Division, which regiment happened to be the 128th. This accounted for me being in line again. So we fought for three days as Fifth Division men, and then the Red Arrows were given a sector of their own far east of the Meuse.[7]

As I said, at eight o'clock we went over the top. Lining up on the lee of the slope we advanced to the top of it, expecting to find the Germans there. To our surprise there was a company of Yanks down in the hollow and on the border of a dense thicket. We recognized our own K Company. They waited for us at the edge of the thicket.

I neglected to say that when we began the advance we drew a new acting corporal. This guy picked out a fellow to be second in command of the squad, but his buddy objected to the choice and the whole squad turned to me and indicated that I was their choice for the place. It is a very lowly position, that of being second in command of a squad, but I still appreciate being chosen for the place by my squad mates on the field of battle—it was no mean compliment.

But when I think of the coward who led us that morn, I think perhaps my job was not much anyway.

We had strict orders to keep in liaison with the squads on either side, but the squad leader surely lost his head because of sheer fright. No sooner had the order been given to advance than he set out at breakneck speed veering to the right at an angle of forty degrees. Within five minutes the other squads were far to the rear and out of sight. Thinking a soldier's first duty was to obey, I kept right behind him rushing as he went way through the woods like a startled deer. I knew he was doing wrong and now know that I ought to have refused to follow him, for he was flagrantly disobeying orders. I shudder to think what would have happened if we had run across some Germans in that woodland, which was nearly a kilometer across.

Luckily we didn't see any, and when we came to the edge of the woods we were the only Yanks near and a profusely perspiring lot even though the day was cold.

To our left was a hollow, but in front of us the hilltop was a plateau. Out there a half kilometer away stood four or five figures looming up in the morning mist with uniforms a bluish green. "Here at last we have found the Boches," thought we, and began to take sight, knowing we could wipe out the whole bunch at one volley before they knew we were near, but the squad leader ordered us not to shoot. So, in an angry mood, one little West Virginian being extremely violent in his language, we slunk back into the edge of the woods to await the coming of our comrades.

Twenty minutes later olive drab figures by the scores suddenly appeared in our rear as though mysteriously sprung out of the ground, but the faces were those of strangers—if I remember correctly they were part of the Second Battalion of the 128th.

Soon an officer appeared and told us that the front ran almost at right angles to what we had supposed and that the men we had wanted to shoot and who were still talking and pointing were Frenchmen and not Germans. Had we shot them, France would have had more officers among her lists of the dead.

At length we espied M Company lying around on the ground down in the hollow more than a half quarter to our left and gladly joined our buddies.

As we didn't move for quite a bit, I took the squad canteens and set out for water with exploring ideas on the side. There was a machine gun somewhere in front that kept up a continual racket like a mighty woodpecker, and just before I got where I could see it a lively little brush took place on the hill just over the way. At the edge of the woods I was in I met a Yank who said that the scrap was the Sixth Infantry going over the top, and that they won out.

Nearby I found German shacks but lately deserted and several fresh dugouts. At the last one of the shacks I found a very small stream of water. I quenched my thirst and tried to fill the canteens, but the stream trickled so slowly that at the end of a half hour I had one and a half canteens of water. So I went back with that, fearing that the company had gone while I was away.

On top of the high hill across the way I descried marching men—they were Germans, about two hundred of them—but a half dozen Yanks marched on the side of the column, so I knew they were prisoners.

Imagine my chagrin and some amusement, too, when twenty minutes later one of our lieutenants was running around like a chicken with its head chopped off getting a detachment ready to resist the enemy coming up the path I had just trod. In vain I told the corporal and a sergeant that they were prisoners—the patrol had to go meet them and verify my statement.

And then the afternoon march began, a long toilsome march, up one of the steepest hills in France and across the plateau on top over ridges, across open fields, through dense woods though with small trees but no trace of our quarry, the Germans. Miles and miles we traveled on and on, not knowing what instant a battle would begin.

At a halt on an open field our squad leader was relieved of his command and a likable fellow named Marlot from the fighting state of Pennsylvania placed in charge of the squad.

Sometimes during the afternoon we "leapfrogged" a part of the Fifth Division engineers and were now surely front liners. Through a thick low woods and we came out above a deep transverse valley. I thought surely the enemy would be here. Many of his shells had passed over and landed near during the afternoon, but that was the only sign of him. The sun was hanging low in the west when we began to descend into the quiet valley. Down it a mile or so to the left was a pretty village. I have since learned that it was Fontaines. On the floor of the valley we encountered some German hoop wire that delayed us a bit. It was all that I ever saw.

On nearing a woodland up a narrow vale we came upon a wounded German; he had been wounded in the head with a fragment of shell and was far gone though still conscious. I have been told that an M Company sergeant shot and killed him as he lay helpless. I hope it is untrue and think it is as I heard no pistol shot. Still if he did it was really an act of mercy, for it would have been next to impossible to carry him back to the hospital.

On the sides of a steep hill we found a few German shanties, and, deploying up and down the hill just as the sun went down, we camped for the night. A rifle shot rang out up the hill, and I knew the strain had been too great for some man and he had shot himself.

In the narrow vale below us were four German 88 guns. The road had ended and they had to be abandoned. The French had played a Masurian Lakes trick on the Boches.[8]

15

Brandeville

Fifty yards below my station on the hillside was a small wooden shanty like the others on the slope. I went down to the shack and inside to see what I could see. The principal attraction within was a piano, and a jim-dandy at that. Evidently it had been brought to brighten the hours of the German soldiers in these wild, wooded solitudes. I tried my hand at playing and, though the instrument had a splendid tone, my many months' loss of practice caused me to be absolutely unable to play a tune. Consequently I did not tarry long. Scarcely had I got back to my camping place when a huge German shell fell at the end of the shanty. They were trying to destroy what they had left.

My bunkie that night was a little fellow named Coffee who had been my bedfellow once before at Romagne. To avoid rolling packs the next morning we did not unroll same that night but made a makeshift bed out of articles we secured from the shanties near, supplemented by our overcoats and raincoats. We slept fitfully.

Up early the next morning we were soon on the march. Half a mile on our way we came to the previous night's camp of the German rear guard. But no enemy was to be seen, and we pressed on through the greatest forest I saw over there, I think. What impressed me most was the huge size of the beeches, towering shapely and tall into the air.

Miles and yet more weary miles we put behind us. A little past noon we halted and ate some iron rations. Coffee did not eat much and gave me most of his share, so I had a fairly good dinner.

Resuming the march, we trailed a narrow-gauge railroad for a ways and came out onto an open field. Here we deployed in squad column, our company being in the second wave. It was here that I noticed how thick the fog was. True, I had known all day that it was foggy, but in the dark woods I had not paid so much attention, and now I noticed that we could see less than two hundred yards ahead of us.

The lieutenant commanding the battalion asked the second in command if he thought it best to send out a patrol and that gentle-man replied, "I would suggest that we go ahead as we are until we find something." I was glad that the advice was accepted, though events proved that the patrol idea was best.

Perhaps you will think it strange that I am not saying much about my company commander. Well, I had very little to do with com-manders, and as I am recording my experiences I left it out. Will say that on all this strenuous march of twenty-five miles through the woods and over as rough terrain as troops usually march, our leader had been Lieutenant Teeter, a likable and brave soldier. I have often wished I had been more closely associated with him.

The march began again. The field was small, and by the time we reached the woods at the far edge we heard the sound of machine guns a little over to the right. I felt in my bones that a battle was on.

Somehow the sounds momentarily grew louder and our marching seemed circularly around the hill somewhat in the direction of the sounds. At length the sharp reports seemed to be coming from the treetops near us. Yes, I was excited, but had good self-control, for I remember stopping to pick and eat a lone juicy blackberry and think-ing of the lateness of the season. A moment later a gray squirrel, alarmed at the machine-gun bullets whizzing through the treetops, ran down a large beech in sight of nearly the whole battalion. He escaped unhurt and even unshot-at, for we were stalking bigger game.

Then we came to the flat top of the hill less than a hundred yards wide. There was a perfect little furor just to the right, where through the fog I discerned an opening that betokened a field. The din was terrible, and my heart was thumping loudly.

Eventually I became aware that the little fellow behind me was saying something to me. I looked around, and my roll legging was strung out nearly the entire length. So I stepped aside and fixed the legging while the squad moved on. This little occurrence may have saved my life, but I wished in a moment that I hadn't stopped. Why? A machine gun opened on me and was clipping the tops of the alderlike shrubs all about me about as high as my head. So I lay prone on the ground behind a little beech tree about ten inches in diameter, thinking it would quit in a moment. But it did not quit, and other guns were chattering now in our front. Then I heard the low trusty bark of the Springfields and knew M Company was in action. There was something about the bark that drew me and I arose to go, thinking to walk half bent and so go under the bullets, but I reckoned wrongly for another machine gun instantly opened on the twigs a little lower down. So I decided to wait longer.

I can never describe this trying situation. I wanted to go on and navigate the twenty yards to the opening ahead of me; I knew my squad was not more than a few yards out in the open; the din was furious, awe-inspiring, terrific. Through my mind constantly ran the thought, "Brave men are dying out there, I ought to be there with them." Three times I got up to go, and every time there was a fresh burst of machine-gun fire, until there were at least six firing right over and around me. To make matters worse some were in front of me, others straight toward the right, so they were cross firing over me, some cutting twigs as high as my head, others whittling them to bits waist high, and one particularly wicked one was tearing the alders not more than two feet from my head. To have done other than lie flat would have been suicide, and I fancy that I was about as flat as a spreading adder, indeed I was as close down as I could get.

How long the uproar of machine guns, rifles, and the punctuating boom of a one-pounder lasted, I cannot say—it seemed an hour, but I imagine fifteen minutes nearer the correct time. And then horror-stricken as I was, I was yet more terrified by a one-pounder shell that flew by me from the right about eight inches above the ground and a foot from the tree on the other side, its trajectory clearly marked by vibrating twigs it had touched. Luckily for me it was on the other side; had it been on my side, you would not have been reading this, for it would have hit my pack and exploded. Dead men don't write diaries.[1]

Suddenly there was a letup in the firing and running olive drab figures entered the woodland, came toward me, and passed me. I recognized my own squad and two others. All was clear now; it was simply too hot to stay out there. I swung in on the rear of my squad and the guns began again, but this time they were shooting about eight feet above ground but might lower any minute. My ammunition belt fell off and the revolver Steen had given me. Foolishly I went back and got it.

Turning again to the rear, I saw my squad had gained on me. A low heavyset man, Warner Davis by name, from West Virginia, ran past me and sat down at the foot of a big beech tree. Blood was streaming from his finger tips. A thought came to stop with him, but as his wound was in the arm I thought it likely wasn't serious. A bit farther I was about to pass a man named Bennett. He called to me to report to his squad that he was wounded. I asked him where his wound was, and he replied that a machine-gun bullet had passed through his ankle. I told him I would stay with him and help him get back to the first aid station.

We were now at the brink of the hill and had just reached a broad path. A machine gun commenced clipping the twigs so close to me that I could have touched them with my left hand. Don't say, "Did you run?" But I couldn't run at all. Bennett, crippled as he was, outdistanced me in half a minute and was at the foot of the hill by the time I got halfway. He knew how it felt to get shot. I have never seen or heard of him since.

The path down the hill was strewn with packs cast off by the Yanks in their flight, nor do I deem it a disgrace to have fled from that fatal field. Since the brow of the hill was passed I did not travel so fast. I came to the railroad near the foot of the hill (narrow-gauge), passed it, and started up the next hill. I heard a frightened voice yelling "M Company, this way" on the hill. I knew one of the lieutenants (dreadfully wounded with mustard gas, it happened) was ahead, but M Company was not. Less than a third was there.

In an open place in the woods a big man with an overcoat on stood, halting the fugitives as they came. He was not in the best of humor about it either, and when one man tried to pass, saying he had a message to deliver, the big man belabored him over the helmet with his rifle. It was clear to me now that though the Americans were worsted in the little fight, the line was still holding. I decided that it would never do to be carried back to the lines at the point of a rifle, so I slipped through the bushes and started back because duty said my place was there. I have been told that the big man was the colonel of the Eleventh Infantry; others have said he was merely a captain of that outfit. Anyway, he was brave and determined.

Back at the railroad, shells began falling among us—there were a number of Yanks around. I dived into the ditch beside the road and met with a comrade of M Company. Don't ask if the shells were German. Our artillery was likely twenty-five miles to the rear.

The buddy I met in the ditch was a little Louisiana Frenchman and the palest man I ever saw. Four bullet prints were on one square inch of his helmet front, his bayonet was shot in two, and a bullet had gone through his rifle stock. Close call, eh? Frenchy was not ready to return to the hilltop, so I set out alone. On the upper side of the railroad I saw one of our corporals bandaging the wounded arm of a comrade. Near him on the ground lay the familiar forms of two more M Company men. They were dying. One was shot in the lower right side; he looked at me with glazing eyes as I passed. And yet I have been told that he recovered. Such are the rumors of war.

As I was going up the hill I noticed that all was quiet on the hill-top. The battle was over, and I visualized the Yanks holding the line at the edge of the woods. The sight of the packs then gave me an idea. I was hungry and there might be reserve rations in the packs, which would be mine for the taking. So I searched and found a couple of car-tons of hardtack and a can of salmon. Stepping into the woods, I ate what I wanted and put the rest in my mess kit for the future.

Desultory firing at the top of the hill told me that some Yanks were there, and I continued my way back to the front. On top of the hill I saw several dead bodies. Poor Davis seated at the foot of the beech was still, in death. Whether he died of his wound, was hit again, or the Germans came and finished him, I'll never know. But there was no sign of M Company or any other company, so I walked cautiously to the edge of the woods. A little field sloped downward, and the sight thereon was enough to make the blood stand still. American soldiers, dead and wounded, but nearly all dead or so nearly as to be motionless, actually lay in windrows, just as the lines had stood when the machine guns had mowed them down. There were fully one hundred fifty in sight, and only a few steps away four dead bodies lay piled across each other as they had fallen. Surely it was a wise providence that had let my legging come loose just at the exact moment to save me.

As I looked over the gory field I saw two live soldiers. They were in a shell hole. I had an impulse to go to them, but caution checked me.

I looked down the hill, straining my eyes through the fog. Some-how there was a blur in the little thicket at the far side of the field a half quarter or less away. I looked again and, horrors, it was a line of German soldiers, not less than two hundred strong, standing or walking about.

It will be difficult to tell my emotions then. Will say that my hair stood on end as it does when I see a snake. I raised my rifle and took deliberate aim. Thinks I, "I can get one now and know I got him." But just as I was ready to pull the trigger I thought of something else: "I can get two at least before they can tell where I am." So I aimed again but failed to shoot again for a pesky thought almost knocked me down. It was, "What if I do kill two or a half dozen and they swarm over the field and kill me, how much will that profit me?" So I decided to let them live and risk chances of living myself.

I looked at the ground at my feet. There was a German ration box. A dead German lay ten steps away. Evidently we had come upon them as they were eating dinner. I looked into the ration box. Part of the grub had been eaten, but some had not been touched. A bottle of milk, a bottle of wine, a small bag of sugar, and another of tiny cakes looked good to me, and I took them along.

Nearby was a German officer's map case. I looked in it. An excellent map of the Argonne-Meuse battlefield, some pencils, and a pen like a fountain pen were the contents. I had heard the propaganda of fountain pens exploding and killing Yanks, but I took it apart to see if it would explode, holding it at arm's length. Nothing happened. I still have the map and the pen.

A hundred yards to the rear I sat down at the foot of a good-sized hickory tree and ate some of the captured grub, particularly drinking some of the milk and wine. And then I arose to go down through the woods that stretched down the field on its western side—the direction the company was going and in which direction I heard voices hallooing.

And here the strangest thing of my army career happened. God certainly was good to me that day! Laugh, if you please, at this, but it is so—as true as truth itself. It was late in the afternoon now; the fog that had persisted all day had turned to a mist, and the bare, thick undergrowth hung thick with the water drops. I started to plunge into the thicket, when I felt that I should not go. I paused an instant and then, thinking it an idle fancy, started on again. This time the impression was much stronger—to the intent that I should not proceed farther—and I paused again. Shaking off the feeling and almost laughing at myself, I hurriedly started forward. This time there was almost if not quite an audible voice from the thicket saying in a commanding tone, "DON'T GO!" Even as I write about it, more than seven years later, cold chills are chasing themselves over me.

I took the warning for what it was worth. If I hadn't you might not have read this. And I unrolled my pack and made my bed under the hickory tree. I did not know it then nor for months later, but my bedfellow of the night before was lying cold and still in death on the gory battlefield not more than one hundred fifty yards away. My shelter half was a good tent and I slept warmly, though in catnaps.

16

Alone in No-man's-land

Perhaps a word about military affairs would be in order. We had chased the Germans a distance of twenty-five miles through an exceedingly rough country, so rough that the artillery could not possibly have gone the way we did. The enemy had had to desert some of their big guns; trenches, except for a terrace ditch around the edge of the battlefield, were things almost forgotten. Verily we were having America's brand of fighting—open warfare. American units advanced through the forests without keeping liaison and even without knowing the other was there.

So it chanced that the Third Battalion of the Eleventh Infantry and the Third Battalion of the 128th had come upon the Germans here at Brandeville at nearly the same time, neither unit knowing the other was anywhere near. It was this element of the Eleventh that was engaged in the battle to our right a few moments before we got in. By a singular chance both battalions were in the same fighting order, K and L companies in the front wave and M and I in the second. Too, and I do not know whose fault it was, perhaps no one's, but we were supposed to be on their right, while we were on their left.

And so it happened that in the thick fog the Eleventh had walked out onto the fatal field on the far side of which were placed a number of machine guns. Consequently, the men were mowed down in heaps. Just why my battalion did the same unless for the purpose of flanking, I cannot imagine. Perhaps, the leaders thought there were no machine guns in our front. This may also account for the bullets coming from the right. The enemy were endeavoring to prevent flanking. Just why my company got nearly abreast the front line unless it went off at a tangent while circling the hill or we came upon the front wave unable to proceed farther, I am unable to say. The right of the company, my part, suffered worst, as the left did not all get out of the woods. I can only say that the slaughter was terrible, the battalion losing about one hundred fifty killed and the other unit as many. M Company's Honor Roll lists the names of nineteen men killed that day, and the chances are that it was done in fifteen minutes. Then the number of wounded was much larger, making our total casualties approximate 40 percent of our numbers. We had at least one man captured, and I think three the correct number. My bunkie, Coffee, of the night before, my good friend Dennis, and my [Camp] Beauregard buddy Arms were all among the slain.

In the neighborhood of thirty of the boys had taken to the rear, and about that number remained on the line. I was alone in the woodland with the Germans less than three hundred yards away.

Shortly after dark I heard American voices. Listening intently, I noted that there were five or six of the men and I decided that they were intending to establish an outpost, as they halted directly between me and the Germans and on the edge of the woods. Shortly, a familiar racket there told me that they had established a machine-gun nest and were trying it out on the Germans. The reply of the enemy started soon, and again the bullets whizzed over me, but the crest of the hill protected me from them, that is, my bed was slightly beyond it and on a gentle slope.

At least eight or ten times I was awake that night. Sometimes it was because of machine guns, of which there were several down to the right, always accompanied by German star shells shot up from their position, which lighted up the whole landscape, not neglecting my corner of the woodland, with a brilliant but sickly light. At other times it was thirst pure and simple that woke me. I had had not a drop of water for more than thirty-six hours (since noon of the sixth). At such times I drank milk from the bottle; when it was gone I would take a sip of the wine, which was deliciously cold and would appease my thirst until I would drop off to sleep again. This wine is the only wine I ever drank in my life and I drank it to stay my thirst for water. Before morning the entire bottleful was gone, but I felt no effects whatever unless my feelings of warmth could be attributed to it. When morning came, wine and milk were gone and thirst still raged.

Just as I finished packing up to move on, a Boche machine-gun bullet cut a small limb from the tree that was my host that night. Queer way of saying "Good morning," was it not?

November 8

The fog was gone, no voice warned me against the woods, and I plunged through the underbrush, hoping to reach my company before it moved, yet dreading another going over the top.

Three hundred yards away I spied figures slipping through the woods in single file. They were Yanks. They halted on the edge of the woods, which was the western terminus this time. I asked them who they were and was told, "K Company, Eleventh Infantry." I asked them if they had stayed near there that night. They replied, "Nearly a half mile to the east." And then I told them about hearing voices in this direction and was told, "There were no Americans in this part of the woods last night."

The truth now dawned upon me. It was Germans I had heard, and a kind Providence had kept me from stumbling upon them in the dark woods. Too, I had slept alone between the lines—in no-man's-land.

From them I learned that M Company was a half mile to the east or perhaps more and that the boys to whom I was talking were going over the top in a few minutes.

As I was leaving, a nice young officer accosted me, asked me some questions, told me I was likely to run across the Boche in the woods, and invited me to join his outfit, saying when the drive was over he would give a statement to me to give my commander telling where I had been and that I would get credit for any services I might render. I thanked him for his kindness, but, as I knew about where my company was, told him I thought I could find it. He did not persist as he might have done. I guess he knew I was sincere in trying to find the outfit or I wouldn't have been on the front line.

I also encountered a chow detail from God knows where in the woods, and as there was to be an over the top decided I was not in a hurry to get to the command.

So I sat down at the foot of a huge beech tree and waited. Pretty soon I heard a few words of command to the company a hundred yards behind me. I heard them scramble out of the terrace ditch and line up and the word given to go. In a few moments there was a rifle shot, and another. I counted up to seventy and then there were too many to count. A machine gun opened, and I knew the valiant Eleventh Infantry boys were having a lively little scrap. The machine gun hushed, there were a few scattering rifle shots, then silence, and I knew our boys had gained the day.

But there was no noise of battle toward the east. I waited and waited, but no sounds came, so I leisurely took up the hunt again, pausing every once in a while to see what I could tell from the sounds.

Back to the place where I had seen the Germans, and looked again, the sun was shining brightly now but no enemy were to be seen. A short distance farther I went back to the edge of the woods and looked again. An American was walking briskly across the field. He stopped to look at a wounded man who moved, then walked on. Evidently the wounded fellow was far gone. I marveled that the walker was not shot dead.

I took an awfully long time to navigate that half mile. The sun had reached its meridian and there had been no fight, nor had I found M Company. In front of me I heard a few rifle shots and determined to go to the company at once, for those shots sounded natural.

I was walking along at a swift pace when suddenly a small soldier walked from behind a clump of bushes. He stopped and gazed at me and I gazed at him. It was Evans. Maybe we were not glad to see each other. It was the first either of us knew that the other had escaped death in the battle. I had found the old outfit. The chief of the runners came by and ordered me to report to Lieutenant King, but I reported to no one and found an old-time buddy in the person of Private King nearby.

The chow detail then arrived, and as I was not very hungry I thought I would let the other fellows have my share. But there was plenty of bread and black molasses for all and I ate some.

Then I inquired for water and was told that none was to be had. But thirst was gnawing away and I was suffering. King was nearly in the same fix I was, so going to the edge of the woods I saw several deep horses' tracks filled with clear water from the rain the night before. It was true that there might be mustard gas in it, but I was willing to risk it, so with my little German canteen cup I began drinking and filling my canteen. A voice from the woods stopped us. Lieutenant King was giving me a welcome back home by bawling us out, telling us that it didn't matter if we were killed but that we ought not to draw the fire of the Germans on good men, meaning the others, of course. This had a great deal of effect on us for we went back into the woods and out again at the end of same and finished quenching our thirst and filling our canteens. I have seldom drunk water that tasted better than this.

Here at the end of the woods we saw blue-coated figures waddling down the hill over to the right. Some of the boys fired on them, but they sent up a flare and we knew they were French.

I had made a discovery while on the front side of the woods. The hills dropped off sheer a hundred feet a little ways in front of us and a splendid valley glistened in the sunlight for miles. I looked at the splendid panorama a long time. Till now I thought we were in a land of small eminences and hollows. Little did I dream that we were on the brink of the rugged escarpment that divided the highlands east of the Meuse from the Woevre Plain.[1]

Soon Lieutenant King was running around like a chicken with his head chopped off. We lined up and, yes, I was just in time to go over the top. The whole battalion went over as one company and was not so large as some companies. I followed a private named Barnes, acting as corporal.

At the brink of the escarpment we spied a town at the steep foot thereof. I was looking out for Germans and watching my step down the precipitous hill. We went in at the back door of a house and out onto the street, down a side street, and out into the open country. No Germans were seen by me, though I have been told they were visible in flight from the top of the cliff about two miles out on the plain.

In a three- or four-acre field on a bench at the foot of the far hillside we found a huge cabbage patch. The cabbages were fine and the patch looked like a drove of cattle had been through when we had passed, it being no uncommon sight to see a soldier with his head half buried in a fine cabbage head.

Brandeville is in a narrow defile eroded from the face of the escarpment. Beyond it is a bold ridge flinging itself in haughty derision at the valley; the end of the ridge is almost a mountain peak lording it over the valleys and plain. Thither we betook ourselves and three-fourths of the way up the ridge dug in under the low fir trees. Brandeville has one of the finest springs I have ever seen, and a water detail soon went back to fill our canteens. While they were gone, enemy planes flew over the village and dropped bombs on the railroad track.

Adams and Atchley of East Tennessee were my bunkies. It was a curious experience to lie in the dugout, listening to the huge shells fall and explode far down in the valley beneath us, and then a moment later feel the mountain quake and tremble from the impact. We were fairly safe ourselves, as it would have been hard for the Germans to have hit us on our steep hillside. It would have had to have been a direct hit or harmless.

After dark the hostile gunners took a notion to hit the depot and a few cars near it out on the plain nearly a half mile away. One of the cars was loaded with explosives, and the persistent gunner kept banging away until a lucky hit ignited the car of explosives and the shelling ceased. The flames spread to another car loaded with hogs, and it wasn't funny to listen to the squeals as the poor things roasted to death.

17

Ecurey

November 9

That sepulchral hour, the second before dawn, found us rudely awakened from a cozy sleep and ordered to roll packs. I venture to say that there has never been a darker night—there could not well be. Seeing no more than a totally blind man, we rolled packs and headed to the rear. Thank goodness, our turn of duty was ended and relief was near.

Winding around the steep hillside, single file, much like burros, we quietly took our way. Once or twice a man made a misstep and slid down the hill fifteen feet. These accidents served to make us cautious, and we wended our way in a snail-like manner, taking an hour to negotiate a half mile.

The first faint streaks of day were beginning to show in the east, we could dimly discern the path, and our gait quickened. We had crossed the valley in which Brandeville is situated and now surmounted the steep hillside beyond. On and on we went until two hours after daylight we camped in the woods beside an old field so much like one near my home that my mental pictures of the two are interchangeable.

For an hour or two we sat around with nothing to do. Finally I decided to take the canteens and go for water. Do you know, I marvel yet at the freedom I had in the advanced regions? And I wonder sometimes how it happened that I never returned to find the company gone and me not knowing which way it went. And the peculiar thing is that usually I did not have permission to go and never once got into trouble for going or missed anything that happened in the company that was worthwhile.

A vision of yellow and faded leaves persists as I think of that trip through the woods with the ground covered with a thick carpet of leaves. The solitude of the forest was depressing after so much noise of battle.

Somehow I struck a dim path that led down a steep hill a mile from the bivouac. Down, down, down I went and thought I had reached the foot of the hill, but, no, there was another one just like it, and when I got to the bottom of this I was at least two miles from the rest of the boys. I found no spring and kept on and on down the narrow valley.

At length I saw an opening in the woods, and a road at its edge, with a German barracks or two nearby. I was kind of skittish about approaching the buildings, but reasoned that probably water was near, and when I saw Yanks about the houses my fears departed.

But it seemed that the Yanks were rather shy about being seen, as several slunk into the house as I approached. I managed to hail one and asked about water. He informed me that there was a good spring flowing through a pipe across the road. I found it and quickly quenched my thirst and filled the canteens.

I remember watching a man or two down the road, one of whom was an officer, and speculating what their business was. And the train road atop the big hill just to the west came in for its share in my interest. I noticed that the two fellows who came out to the spring with me watched the officer with more interest than I. When I started to leave one of the guys asked me in a whining tone if I were going to tell about them being down there. I told them "no," and they seemed much relieved. Till then I hadn't thought much about the reason for their being there but they were stragglers pure and simple, willfully playing out of battle, or in stronger terms deserters. What they would have done had I told them I would report them I do not know, but I wasn't scared of them—such fellows aren't dangerous and they would not have amounted to much in battle anyway.

It was a long toilsome way back to camp as I had to climb the double hill. I had walked at least five miles when I got back and was so tired I could almost have dropped. I had been gone nearly three hours. I noticed when I got back that quite a few of the fellows who had played rabbit on the seventh had got back to the company. Few of them had the countenance to look me straight in the eye. Guess they knew they had run too far.

Two more hours found us packing up to go take over a new sector to the right of the one we had left. Gosh, the officers in command of the big units had forgotten that there is a limit to human endurance it seemed. Surely the battered Third Battalion had done its bit and gone through the mill, but there was more grist to grind. We grumbled, but it amounted to nothing.

It was a long wearisome journey, most of the time winding along the road a short distance back of the brink of the hills. And the distance, in the neighborhood of ten miles, was covered before nightfall. I remember passing my dear friend Banholzer on the road. He was a stretcher bearer and was worn haggard. Did he feel that his time was near as did so many other boys doomed to die? I talked with him a bit for the last time.

Just before dark the road turned to the left, and soon we were winding around the side of the hill, going down it. In the little valley below was the village of Ecurey, and upon the slope above it in the lee of a high hill, were a number of German barracks. Visions of sleeping in a house once more danced in our heads and were made more intense by the sight of Prather and one or two others standing beside the road and smiling as they were watching over cans of chow still warm.

Did we begin eating? Well, yes, but begin is all. For just as we had got a good start orders came to stop eating and resume the march. Hurrying through the village we came to the open country beyond. But we halted at the forks of the roads to learn which way to go. This was on the edge of the plains, and we came face to face with real war again and realized that another trip to the front would be our portion. I have recollections of numbers of Frenchmen going this way and that, of meetings and handshakings it seemed to me uncalled for.

Out on the plain, we deployed in squad column. Again we had a respectable company, though much smaller than before Brandeville. Were we going over the top? No, we were going to stand there, in mud and water shoe-mouth deep, and wait until darkness veiled the land. Then squad by squad we came back to the road and silently took our way up the side of it. The mud was awful, the mud was awful, the mud was awful!

Two miles of this and we came to a village of the plains. It was Peuvillers. We had orders to be quiet as we approached it. So we slipped into its streets and stealthily wended our way down them. Halting beside the silent church I could see enough to know that there were fresh graves in the churchyard. The village was as silent as the city of the dead, and then came the whispered order passed down the line to "Be very quiet." So we tiptoed across the bridge, down the silent street, and not breaking the silence gained the open country once more. A straight muddy road lay before us, and I wondered why we were so cautious if the Germans were far away. Two hundred yards more and we halted on the muddy road. A Frenchman was standing there and began giving instructions to our commander through an interpreter. He said the Germans were just over the hill, rather, top of the slope, one hundred fifty yards away. A Cossack post was near this, relieved by Corporal Mead and two others.[1]

While we were standing there, French soldiers began to bob up in the road and silently pass to the rear. I wondered where they had been but soon found out. They were alongside the highway, and the thicker darkness in the ditches concealed them until they were in the road. The French departed, and we were strung up and down the road as they had been. Atchley and I drew a drainage ditch for our home, and getting into it we lay down to try to sleep, but it was a terrible ordeal—it was the worst night I ever put over.

18

Peuvillers

I wonder sometimes if dear old Atchley in his mountain home in East Tennessee ever tells his friends of that terrible night when he and I were bedfellows, or I might be more explicit if I were to say ditch fellows. To give you an idea of what we suffered, I will say that when we lay down about nine o'clock that night the road was a mess of soft oozy mud at least six inches deep; when we got up at dawn the next morning the road was frozen hard as a bone. To give a further idea of the discomfort of that hotel, will say that the ditch was so narrow that we had to lie down sideways and both lie down at the same time. When one became so cramped and aching that he had to get up and change positions, he had to wake the other and both get up simultaneously. Well, says you, "Did you sleep any?" Sure we did. "Did you get cold?" Rather. "How did you manage to sleep?" Sheer exhaustion forced us to.

We had orders not to pull off our shoes, but I knew I couldn't sleep with those muddy, soaked through and through things on. So I disobeyed orders and set my shoes on the bank of our ditch. My overcoat was likewise soaked because of the several showers of the few days previous, so I laid it alongside the shoes after vainly trying to fit it into our bedding.

And when morning broke, behold the ground was frozen, my coat was frozen stiff, my shoes were like boards. Somehow I eventually worked my way into those shoes. I thought my feet would surely freeze, so, regardless of the Germans who might be seeing me, I got out onto the road and began to dance and hop about with the idea of warming up my icy feet. They tell me that Sergeant Smith, similarly occupied thirty steps down the road, got a Boche bullet through his ankle for his trouble. I did not see this happen or learn that the sergeant was wounded until afterward.

And lest the reader does not happen to look at a calendar to find it out, will say that this cold tenth of November happened to be Sunday, though it looked like any other day of the week rather than the Sabbath.

Though it was foggy, the sun was trying to shine. Peuvillers, a small village of the plain, loomed dimly through the fog two hundred yards to the east. Far beyond and high in the air above the densest of the fog was dimly to be discerned the rugged escarpment where the hilly region quickly descended to the Woevre Plain. The road beside which we were located ran nearly due west for a mile or more. In front was a gently sloping rise that ran back a hundred and fifty yards. Here the Germans were stationed. To our rear was a broad flat plain, through which meandered a brook.

While I was trying to get my feet warm a comrade was busy every few minutes saying that orders had been sent to the kitchen for a good warm breakfast to be served to us at six o'clock. I believed little of this, for it was now seven and no breakfast in view.

And then a little group of men loomed up back on the plain. I shuddered at first, thinking they might be Germans flanking us, but my fears were soon dispelled when I discerned the o.d. uniform. They were marching queerly I thought—they had assumed the battle formation as the point of the vanguard. And when I saw a larger body of Yanks behind them I knew something was going to happen and that soon, too.

While I sat on the roadside and watched them approaching the fog lifted and a whole battalion stood out on the plain. The point of advance had now borne a little to the left but was fast approaching the road and was not more than two hundred yards away from me. Suddenly there was a clatter of a machine gun in their direction and I looked at them to see them lying prone on the ground. One by one they arose and turned their attention to a group of buildings a hundred yards from them and in full view of me. The wicked clatter of the machine gun kept up and the Yanks advanced with nothing whatever to protect them from the bullets.

And then I suddenly realized: "Great Jehoshaphat!" I had been there for an hour fully exposed to the fire of the enemy in those buildings if they had cared to fire, to say nothing of those at the top of the hill. But I had been very complacent even when my comrades had warned me of danger. I guess it was just God's mercy that they didn't kill me.

Somehow I did not see the Yanks rout out the machine-gun nest but am sure they did. My attention was drawn to the new rapidly approaching battalion of Yanks, who manifested great surprise at finding us where they thought they would find the Germans. And here let me say that it seems that M Company was the only Yank outfit along that road that night.

The first wave of the battalion did not stop but went right on toward the top of the hill. I thought something would happen when we got there, but it didn't. The battalion halted just as the second wave reached the road and a C Company man and I had a pleasant chat as we sat on the bank by the road. The battalion leapfrogging M Company was our own First Battalion.

The troops went on, but another battalion was directly behind them. It was the Second Battalion. When it passed we were ordered to get ready to go too. The other companies of the command appeared somehow, and shortly we were on the move.

As we were going up that little hill Steen put me in command of one of the three squads of his platoon. I had followed Steen as corporal in my first over the top. Now, in my last, I was following him again, he as sergeant, I as acting corporal. I guess if the war had lasted long enough I would eventually have been a general but am glad to have escaped that honor, since it would have meant untold hardships for me, to say nothing of the other boys.

It was with some trepidation that I led my squad to the top of the hill. Do you imagine what it would have been if those other two battalions had not been ahead of me? But once I got to the summit, my fears vanished and I experienced the greatest thrill I ever felt in all my army career. There spread out in front of me was a narrow valley destitute of trees for a space of about a quarter of a mile wide and a mile long. It was nearly a half mile to where the clearing in the valley began. To the west was a dense bank of woods, to the east a thinner woodland. Straight across the plain the Yanks were marching, the First Battalion headed for the cleared valley, six hundred meters back of them marched the Second Battalion as unwaveringly as the First, though German bullets must have been flying thick and fast.

Six hundred more meters intervened between the Second Battalion and ours. It was one of the few times I or anyone else saw a whole regiment attacking in battle formation and the audacity of the thing was startling, for the Germans were back in the woods beside the valley and on either side, perhaps.

A few, though only a few, shells were falling, and once in a while I could hear a bullet whistle. Some of our men were hit when a shell fell among the advancing host away over on the right, but I think those were the only casualties of our battalion in the early part of the day. So the regiment marched on with never a halt, the Germans giving back in front of the First Battalion as they had from the top of the hill. I was kept busy keeping just abreast of the company front, which was something new to me, and relaying orders from the company commander, Lieutenant King, to Sergeant Steen. It sounded queer to have a real live lieutenant address me seriously as "corporal."

By and by the company reached a brook that ran through the meadow. It goes by the melodious name of Thurte Theinte. Just at the place where we came to it, it was ten feet across and at least waist deep. I did not like fording it on such a cold morning, so looked to right and left. Directly in front of the headquarters squad, which was headed by Lieutenant King, the brook narrowed to four feet but the water was very swift there. Without thinking a second time I ran up the creek despite a terrific bawling out from the lieutenant, jumped across, and scampered back to my place. Needless to say that every man in my squad followed their leader's example and quickly were marching along again as though nothing had happened. The good lieutenant ceased his eruption when he saw we were back in our places, no harm done, and best of all our clothes dry. He was in the right in bawling me out, but I am still confident that I was in the right by chasing up the brook to a crossing place.

Well, I can't tell it all—how the Germans gave back and back and back until we were a full two miles from where we started and how these devils retired to the woods on either side and knowing that the French on our right and an American regiment on our left were not coming to the attack as they should have, set a trap to catch a whole regiment and came precious near doing so. Indeed, I understand that at one time they were on three sides of us and attempted to come in on our rear, but their nerve failed when a single gun of the 323rd or 324th artillery [regiments] lately assigned to the Thirty-second Division made several telling hits upon them.[1]

Well, for our part we marched and we marched. Bullets whistled over our heads and around us, machine guns popped, cannon boomed near us on the hill to our left, but we did not catch up with the other battalions. I wanted to take my squad and slip up on the cannoneers, Indian fashion, and stop those hated noises, but we went ahead. Then through a wood and across a small brook much like one at home and we halted and lay down.

And then the battle began in earnest. I have a vivid recollection of a glance across an open field with a Yank battalion in skirmish line stretched across it and the field fairly sizzling with bullets. But it was not the plan for us to enter that field until the battalion there had advanced a certain distance, so we sought what protection we could and waited. We were in the midst of another inferno but not making part of the noise. But the Germans knew we were there, as the whiz-bangs they launched at us from the east testified. One of these hit a treetop over me and broke it out, nearly frightening me out of my wits.[2]

After a long time, it seemed an hour, we had orders to retreat our steps. We took position in a ditch that the French must have dug for military purposes years ago. It was just right, position, depth, and all, and I could see no other reason for its being there. The uproar gradually lessened. We could see nothing of the battle now, for we were in the deep woods. I began to wonder if we would have to spend the night in that forsaken ditch.

Presently we caught a glimpse of a company filing along toward the rear close by our position. And then there was another and another. I wondered why they were doing this but soon found out. That is, I found out what they were doing and will tell you now, though at the time of my narrative it was dark to me.

The powers that were, seeing that we were in the predicament we were and that the elements on either side of us could not come up in time to aid us, gave orders for us to retire to the position we had left that morning. Since the Third Battalion had come up last, we were to hold fast while the other two battalions went to the rear, and then we went back. But I'll tell the world it was not funny to retire with the Germans closing in on the rear.

Finally, it came our time to start. We went in order as long as we went through the woods, and we went through them farther than we did coming up. When we reached the edge of the woods a full half mile from our hilltop and saw the state of affairs, we broke ranks, became a disorganized mob, every fellow for himself and the Germans take the hindmost.

I often tell people about this episode. I tell them I led a squad over the top that day and that when I got back to the road by Peuvillers, I was alone, which was the truth. Usually there are exclamations of "Did they all get killed?" And I calmly answered, "No, they all out-ran me." That was true also.

Somehow my Pennsylvania friend Davis and I got together. When we got to the little creek with the funny name, the fellows were plunging in and wading across. Davis and I happened to the extreme good luck to walk up to the brook right at a footlog, so we got across dry-shod. 'Tis said that our major took his time and hunted a footing on the way up but that when he got back to it he plunged in and waded across waist deep.

Despite the facts that the Germans were closing in behind us, that bullets were whistling over to our left, and most of the Yanks were ahead of us, my comrade and I found that we just must sit down for a few moments' rest. I had left nearly all my belongings except a couple of blankets where I had started that morning, even including my overcoat. So I didn't have much of a load, though I was exhausted. Where we stopped was so muddy that it took us both to get Davis's pack out of the mud when we started on. The few moments' rest helped us wonderfully.

Over to our left was a smooth expanse of water, probably shoe-mouth deep, and covering an acre perhaps. A Yank or two was wading through it. Suddenly a Boche machine gun opened upon them. The bullets kicked up the water ten feet behind them. Of course they ran, the bullets picking up the water ten feet behind them no matter how fast they ran. I couldn't suppress a smile as I watched the occurrence, and I thought that the German who was aiming the gun was probably having a rare bit of fun at their expense. It lacked lots of being funny to the runners, though they got away safely.

Somehow Davis and I bore to the right in going back. Shortly we came to a German cannon that had been abandoned that morning when the Yanks advanced. About the time we got there, bullets began to "whew, whew" around us. We hid behind the steel plate built to protect the gunner. I noticed that American packs and overcoats were stacked in profusion around and on the cannon—cast off as the boys passed it, perhaps some even when we were going up that morning. When the bullets ceased, I began to search the packs, thinking to salvage something to eat, but Davis thought more of his hide than he did of his stomach, so he went on and left me.

Soon I found a can of tomatoes and felt well paid for my trouble. And then I saw a good-looking overcoat lying atop the cannon and decided I should take it along in place of the one I had left and which someone else might appropriate when it got dry. This overcoat is the olive drab overcoat that I wear yet. It is a real souvenir of the battlefield, and I would not part with it willingly.

When I started on, there were few Yanks near me, indeed none within two hundred yards, though there were some as far from the road as I. The Germans had halted at the edge of the woods, but I was certainly within plain sight of a lot of them.

Soon bullets whistling within a yard or two of me showed me that I was a point-blank target for them. I lay down and the firing ceased, I arose and started on and it began again. When I lay prone the missives stopped again. Wonder if they thought they had hit me. Needless to say that I traveled faster when I traveled but I was really unable to run. Again the bullets cut the air around me, and I stumbled over the first terrace at the foot of the hill and lay panting but reasonably safe from the bullets. While there I noticed that there was something hard in one of the breast pockets of the overcoat, which happened to be under me. Upon investigation, oh, boy, I found a can of salmon, and I knew I would eat again if the pesky Germans would ever let me get to the top of the hill, which seemed a long ways off yet.

But wonderful to say the Germans did not fire at me again even when on the skyline of the hill, and I sought the drainage ditch where I spent the night before. A huge shell crater was in the road where I had danced about in warming my feet.

They tell me that one of the last of the fellows coming over the hill was walking along unconcernedly. Suddenly he became panic-stricken and began to run forward, calling out the name of his company. These outcries were hushed forever when a huge shell fell beside him and blew him to smithereens. Could it be that he had a warning of his fate? I am sure he could not have heard the shell coming. You never hear a bullet or a shell that hits you, you know. The missile always out-travels its noise.

The road now was a seething mass of olive drab soldiers. There seemed to be no discipline or order whatever among them. Morale was a thing forgotten. We had had too much of the bloody business of war without a respite. Yet the whispered dread of an attack on the road by the Germans nerved us all to be able to resist some more, and I will tell the world that the Germans would have had more than they contracted for if they had tried to budge us therefrom, for we were now really in a fighting humor and would have fought a good scrap without an officer in a mile. Of such a spirit is great America made!

Officers came down the road calling out for the First Battalion to shift down the road. Some went, but many of that brave battalion were lying cold in death two miles toward Vittaville where the high tide of the morning went to. It had suffered heaviest in that day's fighting.

I ate my tomatoes, having to divide with two perfect strangers in order to get a knife to cut the can. But I saved my salmon until I found Davis later in the day, and then we had a feast. However, I had another adventure before then. Just across the road from my position was an acre or two of turnips. The plants were small, but many Yanks were there, pulling up and eating the raw turnips. I decided to join them. Scarcely had I got there when the hateful old "whew, whew" of enemy bullets sounded close to my ears. It had got terribly old to me, and I actually took time to study whether to lie down again and avoid them or to stand there and let them get me as they seemed determined to do. Glory be, those were my last bullets to dodge!

In the afternoon M Company was placed on the south side of the road in the narrower ditch there, perhaps to scatter the battalion out more. About four o'clock by sun time, as old Sol was shining brightly, I was sitting listlessly on the side of the ditch deriving all the warmth from the sunshine I could, when suddenly a German airplane flew down the road at an elevation of not more than fifty feet, I judged.

When right over us he fired his machine gun, and almost instantly a shell fell beside the road but on the far side from me.

I must thank the Germans for my shelter this time. A stout bridge spanned the ditch a few feet from me. It was newly constructed of oak logs about twelve inches in diameter quartered, and those covered with earth to a depth of a foot. Did I crawl under the bridge? Foolish question. A corporal took refuge with me there. I felt safe from flying pieces of shell, but what if one had made a direct hit? The shells banged away and boomed and exploded with the most hideous noise until I was sure the whole company must be killed, to say nothing of the other three companies of the battalion. And from the noise the shells surely were twelve inches.

When the noise ceased, the corporal and I crawled from our rendezvous. The most awful silence reigned and men were moving about as if it were a dream. Everything seemed uncanny and unreal. Four men were dead, one of them blown to bits, and four were wounded. The corporal without a word took up his belongings and made for the rear. He had had enough of war. He didn't invite me to go along. I looked across the little flat valley between me and the village. Poison gas was drifting over it about a foot deep, and perfect streams of Yanks were making their way to the safer country in the rear. No one tried to stop them. It seemed as if everyone was his own boss now and if he chose to desert he could. Morale was a thing not possessed by the soldiers now.

I had to smile in the midst of tragedy when I realized from the shell holes that the shells that had caused so much damage and had killed four men within thirty feet of me were one pounders instead of twelve inchers.

I resumed my seat on the ditch bank. Shortly Corporal Mead began calling for two men to help carry a wounded man to the first aid station. There were many closer than I, but I offered my services. Thinking we would be gone only a few minutes, we left our rifles. I never saw mine again.

Halfway to the first aid station, which was in a dugout on the edge of Peuvillers, furious German shells began to scream by us, to hit near us, and to explode, releasing great quantities of poison gas. We put down the wounded man, who donned his mask, and took refuge in a corridor of a house near, putting on our masks as soon as we could, but that was too slow, for each of us got a pretty bad whiff of the gas, one of the fellows probably drew compensation because of it, and for months my lungs seemed raw. Even yet, whenever I have a cold, I have that same burning, raw sensation in my chest.

But the shelling ceased and the gas abated a bit, though not a great deal, and we picked up our wounded man and went on with our masks on. Believe me, that is just about as hard work as I care to do.

At the first aid station a new matter awaited us. The doctor came out of the dugout that served for the purpose and in a few words told us something to this import. "I have a badly wounded man here, his ankle is practically shot in two. We have stopped the blood by means of a tourniquet. He must be rushed back to the regimental first aid station. I was just on the point of sending someone up to the lines to get a detail to take him back. You men are here. I'll just commandeer you to take him and report the matter to your company commander."

Glad to be of service, and any change from the hateful life on the roadside being welcome, we picked up the man and started. The sun was now rapidly declining and would soon be down. Two miles of dreary, muddy, shell-swept plain lay before us, the station being in the little village that nestled between the cliffs on the brow of the rugged escarpment.

The road was half knee-deep in mud all the way and often deeper, many persons were going to and fro along it, therefore the danger of shells was greater there, so we chose a route across the fields where the black mud was only shoe-mouth deep.

But ah, that trip! I shudder sometimes now when I think of it. The stretcher was a bit of poultry wire across a door frame that had been used for a German bunk. It was unhandy, the man was nearly a two hundred pounder, the mud was deep and troublesome, and we in our enervated condition hardly equal to the task. We were lucky in having a D Company man along with us so that we could change up. Too, we had to rest frequently and long to be able to get there at all. And such patience the wounded man had, always thinking of us and our hard work instead of himself.

The sun went down and we toiled on in the thick darkness. We were dog tired, I perhaps more enervated than the others. I was so far gone that I did not in the least resent it when one of the noncoms cursed me because I wanted to rest again when in sight of our goal. The hours had ticked by while we were coming the two miles, and when we with a sigh of relief laid our burden down at the door of the first aid station it was nine o'clock.

So there we were, two miles from the company, hardly enough vim left us to find a place to stay that night, let alone returning through the mud to the horrible ditch by the roadside, so we gladly followed the lead of the corporals to a shanty high up on the hill-side, which though already occupied by some 125th Infantry men still had room for the five of us, and the boys already there, largely Virginians, made us welcome.

19

Armistice Day

Can I forget the night of November 10? It was the second night in seven weeks I had spent under a roof. The kindly Virginia boys of the 125th Infantry will long linger in my memory. There were others, but I remember best the boys from the Old Dominion. We deemed it a rare privilege to be allowed to stay by the stove in those German barracks occupied by our comrades in arms the 125th Infantry, and many were the trips I made to the outside for a handful or two of wood. The feeling of warmth was most welcome after I had known the pinch of cold so long.

One by one the other boys happened to the good luck of getting taken into bed with the fellows of the 125th until I was left sitting by the stove and basking in its rays. Then drowsiness overcame me and I slept but how long I do not know. I awoke to find the room dark, the fire out, and my limbs numb with cold. I kindled another fire, brought in more wood, and was soon back in the land of dreams. Three or four times the experience recurred. Once a 125th private woke up and divided a night lunch of hardtack with me. For it I am still grateful.

About 4:00 a.m. I awoke, rebuilt the fire, and in so doing made enough racket to wake up a Virginia sergeant in the next room, who proceeded to bawl me out. I paid no attention to this, and soon the sergeant came in to share the warmth with me, and half apologize for his haste.

Finding I was from the 128th, he began to talk about how McCoy shot folks off duty. It was plain he considered me a deserter, and I did not have the energy to explain or resent it. I knew our dear Colonel McCoy would not have anybody shot. I knew, too, that he had to go back to the hospital, I believe, for an operation. I knew also that the then commander, Lieutenant Colonel Mayer, was too busy shooting

Germans to have an American shot. When the sergeant finally learned that I had helped bring back a wounded man, he apologized for his suspicions.

Our hosts rolled packs at daybreak saying that a certain major was moving in at seven o'clock. We did not stay to welcome him. The corporals decided that we ought to visit the company kitchen before we went back to the front. Needless to say that it was unanimously agreed to. It took some time for us to find the kitchen. Stumbling upon it about eight o'clock, we were given a dandy meal consisting largely of rice. It was the first full meal I had eaten and the fourth time I had tasted food in a week.

While engaged thus, some Frenchmen similarly occupied just across a glade from us took a fit. They were eating away when suddenly each jumped up, and of all the hugging and kissing they did it. Then they yelled "Vive la France!" and other things. They sat down and drank wine from their canteens, they ate a few bites, but were soon up and cutting didoes again. In the midst of their deliriums suddenly they paused and yelled at us: "La Guerre fini! Boche parti, toute d'suite!" ("The war is over! The Germans will leave, right away!")

We were pleased, but not enough to put on a kissing bee. We didn't believe it anyway, for we had heard so much of such stuff that we thought it was only a veil to hide a gigantic "over the top." In a few minutes the mess sergeant came and said the news was so.

I guess the remainder of the breakfast was good, but I hardly remember finishing. Still I did not believe it, though wave after wave of Yankee yells were resounding over the hills and though a captain had ridden down the winding hill in an auto, leaning from the car yelling at everybody he saw, "Boys, it's over!" Were not such expedients often resorted to when an attack was to be made? Had not the 128th attacked the day before, and was not the 125th now lying over the way on the alert and expecting to be put into the line any moment? Was not the report only to encourage the 125th?

The acting top sergeant had come around soon after we were busy with breakfast and gruffly ordered that we get through hurriedly and go back to the lines. While studying over the good news I did some tall thinking. It was then about 8:30, firing would cease at 11:00, it would take at least an hour and a half to negotiate the distance out across the muddy, fire-swept zone to the lines. And I began to wonder if it would be worth risking my life at every step of the way merely to stay in the lines an hour. I came to the conclusion that I would not go until I saw whether the war closed or not. If it ended, I would go without danger; if it did not end, I would return to my post of duty, dangerous though it would be in the extreme. The reader can judge for himself. I guess I shirked duty for two hours and a half. I let you judge whether I was doing wrong or acting with prudence. I am inclined to the latter opinion.

But the gruff sergeant! To get away from him I slipped around the corner of a German-constructed shanty nearby. Five or six men, all strangers, were seated around a good fire. They welcomed me to a seat with them, and there at the end of that house, situated in a sheltered cove far up the slope of the hill and near the road that winds up from Ecurey, I spent the remaining hours of war.

A mule skinner or two, a private or two, and a gunner from the 323rd Artillery then attached to our division were my companions. The gunner, on the sick list, was decidedly the most talkative one in the crowd. Those two hours were tedious, filled with the small talk of army life; speculations to the truth of the report; disbelief; speculation if it was true; talk of what we would do, if true; hope for a homegoing, and every little bit someone would come by with more news—the thing grew stronger as the minutes passed. Ever and anon a wave of cheering would sweep over the 125th on the hill across the way. It seemed sometimes as if the cannonading was lessening, then it would break out again. But many times before when there were rumors of peace, the guns would still for a minute or two. Once or twice that morning it happened so, but began again. Finally, between ten and eleven, we became aware of regular shots being fired by guns just to the north of us; swiftly the news came that our artillery was firing a farewell—forty-eight shots, one for each state in the Union. Shortly before eleven they ceased and silence reigned there, but the detonation continued elsewhere.

The minutes ticked away, and firing was slower. We almost held our breath as the time neared. The hand of the gunner's watch was on the verge of pointing to eleven, the far-flung battle line was silent, and we were breathless with expectancy, when over to our left loud explosions of bursting shells rent the air. Immediately a clatter of guns arose and the hand of the watch was past eleven. Was the watch wrong or the report false? We believed the latter.

Lost in a deep study of how we had been duped and my perilous journey I must now undertake across the wicked plain to the outfit, I was aroused from my reverie by the gunner exclaiming, "Listen boys, everything's quiet as the grave."

Sure enough, from far west in a wide arc to distant southeast, where had been a continual din, was stillness reigning supreme.

But we waited some minutes like we had often before to make sure that the din would not begin again. This time the quiet continued and our party joyfully broke up, I to go back to the kitchen. Many faces on that side of the house now wore a broad side that for weeks had known only the scowl of battle. None indulged in extravagant merrymaking, however, for we did not know but that the guns would begin any minute.

One man in this crowd bet another twenty francs at fifteen minutes to eleven that the war would not cease, saying he hoped he would lose but feared he would win. In paying it he remarked he had never more gladly lost a bet.

And the top sergeant! Not gruff any more, he was all smiles now. While I was eating dinner he came around and wanted to know if any of us were going to the lines. I told him I was and was instructed to help take the chow up to the company, to which I readily agreed.

The night before had been rainy and all morning the clouds had been a sodden gray, but as the chow detail went through the village of Ecurey the sun burst through the clouds and shone with dazzling rays full upon Old Glory hoisted from the doorway that housed the headquarters of some outfit, probably our regiment. Now I knew that the war was over and in the depths of my soul, fervently, I murmured, "Gott sei dankt," but why I should have said "thank God" in German I have never been able to figure out.

Glad, but still so benumbed in mind that I could not realize the fullness of the meaning of victory, I thought of all the possibilities and of how, barring mishaps, I could go home, but then I thought of my dear buddies fallen in battle and of one in particular, and I said to Hughes who walked beside me, "If only Shirey could go back with us." And he murmured, "Yes."

And little Evans! He had stumbled into a shell hole on one of our night marches and had sprained his ankle badly. Painful though it was he crippled along and kept with the company until Lieutenant King, commanding the company, noticed his injury, the ankle being swollen to twice the normal size, and ordered him back to the kitchen.

And that muddy expanse out toward Peuvillers. Instead of a man or two here or there or a small group spaced five spaces apart and the whole scattered over the fields, a string of Yanks, some going one way and some another, lined the side of the road.

Halfway to the lines a general's car was stuck in the mud, and well stuck. Exactly at that spot our detail met another chow detail and some officers commandeered us to help get the car out. Quickly men swarmed out until there was no room for any more to touch the car. I was not quick about it and seeing I was not needed got back on the bank of the road. On the opposite side stood the general, arms folded and with a far-off look in his eyes, utterly oblivious to the men tugging at his car. I knew that perhaps this was the closest he had ever been to the lines, and I guess the devil whispered a little in my ear. Leastways, I took up the same pose the general had, and thus thought, "Oh, yes, it won't be long until we get back home, and I'll be just as important as you then." Wonder, if he had known my thoughts, if he wouldn't have had me shot at daybreak.

Unable to extricate the car, one of the men told the general he would go get a team from the engineers and pull the car out, so we went on to the company.

In that broad meadow near Peuvillers, through which runs the winding brook and on the south side thereof, we found what was left of a well-nigh destroyed company. Steen, now the ranking sergeant, came to the chow detail and asked if any of the men who carried the wounded man back the night before were present. When I told him I was one, he wrote my name in a little book and said, "That makes thirty-one."

"Thirty-one what, sergeant?" I asked.

"One officer and thirty-one men on duty today," he replied.

We had had three officers and 246 men when we left Chatonrupt, had been sent two officers and 39 men as replacements, thus making a total of five officers and 285 men, not counting a few others who came back from the hospital. Yet notice our strength on Armistice Day!

In the open meadow with blazing bonfires the company lined up for chow, where only a few short hours before it would have been suicide. I could not help being nervous and look occasionally for the Germans to open fire on us again.

I sat by a bonfire studying deeply. I looked up and a pale, trembling man recognizing me said, "Banholzer got it, this morning."

I recognized my friend Cumpston from West Virginia. He told me the painful news of the death of my buddy Banholzer, from Sewanee, Tennessee. As stretcher bearers they had worked all night carrying back the wounded and had heard the glorious news of peace. Cumpston had suggested that they not return to the lines until firing ceased, but Banholzer insisted on going back. Halfway up and less than two hours before "Cease firing," a shell exploded near him, and a small fragment entering one temple and passing out the other killed him instantly.

I was distressed at hearing of his passing under such circumstances and the more so when I remembered his words at Cheppywald. "And if I were to get killed the last day of the war, I never would get over it."

And the sergeant picked me up on a detail to help get the general's car out of the mud. In vain I told the sergeant that a team would come to get it out; he listened, but said, "It's my orders." We started and I noticed it must have been retribution for having treated the general so, that I would have to help get his car out after all, and I resolved not to mistreat any more generals. The team beat us to the car, pulled it out while yet we were a long way off, and I was spared the humiliation of helping.

The bright sun of the afternoon and the sereneness of the vicinity decided me to go back to our position of the afternoon before to get my belongings. The road was as near the German position as ours and I did not trouble to ask Steen if I could go, and though nervous I knew I needed the things I had left. All were gone, even my rifle. Someone had appropriated my revolver, blankets, and other property.

As night drew on I looked for a home for the night. Every little pup tent was full and one of the boys said, "Baker, we would let you stay with us but we have four already." There is none too much room

for two in a pup tent, so I knew it would be crowded. So in company
with some others, just at nightfall, I wended my way across the plain
to a German barracks a half mile in the rear, returning with three or
four bed sacks filled with shavings and a couple of inch planks. The
planks I laid on the ground to keep the bedding from getting wet,
and two of the bed sacks I used for cover.

Chow at 9:00 p.m. was the only army function, but there was one
thing to happen we had not anticipated. Hardly had the sun disappeared from view when a rocket arose from the German line. I shuddered, thinking it might be a signal for an attack, that the armistice
might have been only a ruse to get us off our guard. Soon another
rose down the line, and then another. Evidently the German line
was up to something, and when the number of rockets increased the
Yanks were all staring that way wondering what was going to happen. Suddenly it dawned upon us that the Germans were celebrating because of the close of war.

And those fireworks! Folks may prate of a pyrotechnic display, but
I never expect to see a more magnificent one than the Germans put
on that night. Beginning like the first drops of a summer shower the
rockets and flares increased in numbers as the darkness increased,
and I am sure every Boche soldier participated in the display.

I wish I could describe it to you. The rockets were all colors
almost and shades and combinations of colors, red, green, yellow,
orange, blue, pink, and white. To the best of my recollection one
rocket would have a green light and a red, another an orange and a
blue, and so on. The whole land was livid with color, and they
would shoot up nearer to us than we dreamed the Germans to be
and the line of fireworks was as far as we could see either way. The
French too added a bit of zest to it by sending up rockets as beautiful, but they were over to the east. At the height of the celebration
they set a huge bonfire high on the brow of the rugged escarpment
back near Ecurey.

And the Yanks? Oh, no, we did not participate. There was not a
flare or a rocket to be found in the whole battalion. Our only illumi-
nation was the light of the campfires in the meadow, but we watched
and enjoyed what the others did. The victory was ours, but the Germans were celebrating and the olive drab figures with stolid faces
looked on. Never before in all the history of the world had a whole

army surrendered, thus never before was such a glorious victory recorded in American history that the army of the enemy should capitulate on the field of battle.[1] Now we were going home, the war of our generation had been won, and we had acquitted ourselves well.

Sometimes my friends asked me, "Didn't you shoot your guns to celebrate?" At such times I almost wish I did swear as I could not express my feelings otherwise. Of course we didn't! That's what we had wanted stopped for weeks. Seven long weeks, day and night, we had heard the din, and what we wanted most of all was silence. Had we started shooting, it might have meant a resumption of hostilities.

Many times have I heard it said, "We ought not to have stopped the war, we ought to have gone on to Berlin and torn up their country some, too." Heartless wretch to think such, much less speak it. A thousand American boys were being killed every day and other thousands injured for life. Who would want that to continue, especially in view of what we got out of the war?

And what did we get out of the war? Fifty thousand graves is the biggest item.

By and by the celebration began to tire, rockets became fewer, and I, tired of standing to watch the display, sought my improvised couch. Shortly it began to rain. And there, with the Germans only three hundred yards away, with the four American boys killed on the road the day before lying as they were slain, with the battalion by peaceful campfires for the first time in weeks, I lay and thought of all that had passed and was present and might come in the future.

And with the sodden earth beneath me and sodden clouds above me, with skies weeping as it were over the useless slaughter, I slept by the blazing bonfire and dreamed of the Long, Long Trail that wound westward and ever westward and finally ended at that best of all places—home.

Notes

1. Chatonrupt

1. A Chevaux Limited was a French boxcar, marked to carry eight horses or forty men. For years after World War I the parades of veterans included reproductions of the small freight cars, the forty-and-eights.

2. Army food often was unattractive, but complaints went beyond that. Veterans complained about lack of food, and rations were indeed short; for the level of physical exertion required of them, the men did not get enough to eat.

3. Barns and haymows were the usual billets—the French word became current in World War I. Officers received billets in houses.

4. The first battle of the Marne was the opening battle of the war, in which the German Army lunged into France after the invasion of Belgium, the latter called for by Germany's Schlieffen Plan, named for Count Alfred von Schlieffen, a chief of the German general staff. The plan anticipated an envelopment of Paris. The Germans were stopped at the Marne and retreated but remained in northern France and continued to occupy almost all of Belgium. The second battle of the Marne opened on July 15, 1918, with a German attack, which was repulsed a day later and followed by a Franco-American attack on Soissons beginning July 18.

5. The table of organization for a company of two hundred and fifty men called for one captain, one first lieutenant, and four second lieutenants each assigned to command a sixty-man platoon. Each company had a top sergeant supervising four sergeants (one for each platoon). Each squad of eight men had a corporal.

During World War I the army underestimated the need for company-grade officers (that is, captains and below; field-grade officers were majors and above). For the entire army, at home and in France, the numbers of officers reached two hundred thousand. But the attrition rate—killed and wounded—for company-grade officers was high, and even with new officer training camps that turned out officers in three months ("ninety-day wonders"), there never were enough. In a single action in the Meuse-Argonne a brigade of the Fifth Division lost forty-three out of forty-seven newly arrived second lieutenants.

2. Lavoye

1. The men of the Thirty-second were staying close to their billets because of the imminence of the Meuse-Argonne, which opened Thursday, September 26.

2. Frank R. McCoy graduated from West Point in 1897 and served in General Pershing's headquarters before going with troops as commander of Baker's regiment. During the Meuse-Argonne he was promoted to brigadier general and commanded one of the Thirty-second's two infantry brigades. During the 1920s he served as the army's representative in fractious Nicaragua, where the bandit Augusto César Sandino was attempting a revolution against the United States–recognized government in Managua. In 1931–1932, McCoy was a member of the League of Nations–sponsored Lytton Commission, which sought to determine responsibility for the incident along the South Manchuria Railway that precipitated Manchuria's occupation by Japanese troops and establishment of the Japanese puppet regime of Manchukuo. Too old for active service in World War II, Major General McCoy presided over the Far Eastern Commission that oversaw American policy in East Asia after that war.

3. French rains, of course, were like those of any other country, but men of the AEF were in northern France in late September, a portion of Europe far removed from the latitude of most of their home states. The rain was to be almost constant during the forty-seven days of fighting in the Meuse-Argonne.

4. Camions were the trucks driven by Annamese, belonging to the French Army.

5. Iron rations were the same as field rations—hardtack and corned beef.

6. Soldiers in France quickly picked up rudimentary French.

7. Open-order formations, usually known as extended-order, were necessary in attack to prevent enemy fire, artillery or machine-gun, from decimating entire ranks. The close-order drill so often resorted to in training in the United States was, as Baker wrote, of little use. It looked good in parades.

8. Movement of troops into the front line of the sector between the Meuse River and the Argonne Forest in the days preceding the attack on September 26 was by night, with all road traffic confined to darkness. During the day men stayed in forests or inside village houses and barns, with the purpose of persuading the Germans that the main attack of U.S. troops would be fifty kilometers to the east, from the German salient just taken (on September 12–16) at St. Mihiel, or else from the west in the adjoining sector of the French Fourth Army. The ruse worked, for not until the last day or so, when it was too late, did German divisions in the Meuse-Argonne sense that the AEF was in front of them.

9. The able commander of the Thirty-second Division, General Haan, was well known for drilling troops, doubtless a prime reason for his division's success in battle. After the war he gave a lecture in Madison, Wisconsin, entitled "The Division as a Fighting Machine."

3. A Long Night March

1. This could not have been poison gas. At the beginning of the Meuse-Argonne battle and through October the AEF did not release gas against the German enemy, through canisters or shells; division commanders believed that if they employed gas they would encounter retaliation. The German Army did not hesitate to use gas against the Americans. The employment of gas by the U.S. Army did not occur—except against German artillery positions in the heights of the Meuse, above Verdun—until the American attack beginning November 1, when the army used it in copious quantities.

2. Reference to trenches shows the way in which Baker trained—in trench warfare. He would encounter trenches, often unused, parts of them caved in. The Germans used them occasionally in 1918, protected by rows of staked barbed wire, but relied on machine guns and especially artillery.

3. These would have been guns of the French Fourth Army.

4. First Day of the Meuse-Argonne

1. The preparation fire of three hours opened at 2:30 a.m. A rolling barrage, behind which the infantry moved out, commenced at 5:30.

2. O.d. was olive drab, the color of army issue.

3. The American attack was with nine divisions, equal to eighteen of the Anglo-French and more of the depleted German divisions. In World War I this attack was not as large as Baker believed, for the first attack of the German offensive of 1918 consisted of dozens of divisions. September 26 was sunny, a bright autumn day, but one of the very few such days in the Meuse-Argonne.

4. After the war Baker read the book on the Meuse-Argonne by the military writer Frederick Palmer, whose word for the central ridge of the battlefield was the whaleback. Baker erred in his statement about the Twenty-sixth Division, which had not yet arrived from St. Mihiel and would not attack in the heights of the Meuse until October 29; the Twenty-ninth Division crossed the Meuse on October 8, supported by the Thirty-third.

5. General Pershing's four veteran divisions (the First, Second, Twenty-sixth, and Forty-second) had spent the winter of 1917–1918 in France. The other divisions arrived during the spring and into the summer of 1918. The Second had been with the French Fourth Army and did not enter the line in the Meuse-Argonne until just before the attack of November 1.

6. KPs were kitchen police, detailed to assist cooks.

5. Bivouac and March

1. The Rainbow, or Forty-second, Division comprised National Guard troops from twenty-six states and the District of Columbia. It was named

"Rainbow" by Douglas MacArthur, a major in the war department in 1917 who became successively the division's chief of staff, Eighty-fourth Infantry Brigade commander, and division commander. The Forty-second did not enter the line until the night of October 11–12 and remained until replaced by the Second Division on October 30–31.

2. The Germans had pulled back, for the most part, and were not driven out of trenches because World War I became a war of movement in which reliance was on artillery and machine guns, with occasional trenches joined together or fronted by barbed wire.

3. The Twenty-sixth Infantry was one of the four regiments of the First Division. The First took over the line of the Thirty-fifth Division on the night of September 30–October 1. Its casualties in subsequent days were 7,520, including 1,594 dead. The First took back the territory the Thirty-fifth had lost in a retreat on September 29, Montrebeau Woods and the village of Exermont above it. The division's left regiment, the Sixteenth, took Fléville on the Aire River, which flanked the entire German line in the Argonne Forest.

4. The Thirty-second Division relieved the Ninety-first and Thirty-seventh divisions in the Fifth Corps on the night of September 30–October 1.

6. In Support

1. It was October 4, 1918, and Baker was watching the beginning of the AEF's second attack in the Meuse-Argonne—the first opened September 26. There were two more attacks before the end of the battle and the end of the war, October 14 and November 1.

2. The Ninety-first Division had been the left division in Fifth Corps, relieved by the Thirty-second.

3. "Corn-wully," usually known as corn-willy, was corned beef.

4. The advantage of a reverse slope, well known to all infantrymen, was that it protected troops from incoming shells.

5. The shells must have been no larger than eight-inch. Artillery regiments of the AEF were equipped with three-inch guns (the so-called French 75s, equal to German 88-mm) and six-inch (155-mm) guns. Larger French guns were mostly eight-inch. The battleship rifles of a contingent of U.S. Navy gunners, transported on flatcars, were fourteen-inch, but the German Army did not field guns of such caliber.

8. In the Harness Lodge Woods

1. The rule in the Meuse-Argonne was to make reliefs at night, for alerting the Germans would have been foolhardy.

2. Each member of the AEF carried two dog tags bearing his name on a chain around the neck. In burying the dead, it was customary to remove one. Thus, it was possible to use mass graves.

3. James Oliver Curwood wrote dozens of novels of adventure set in Alaska.

9. North of Cierges

1. French 75s, three-inch guns.

2. The Germans kept batteries on the heights of the Meuse to the east of the river until after the AEF attack on November 1. The batteries commanded positions of troops in the Third Corps on the right of the Meuse-Argonne line, but it is unlikely they could reach into the Thirty-second on the left side of the Fifth Corps.

10. Over the Top

1. This was the third of the four attacks in the Meuse-Argonne. The interesting point is that the Thirty-second, which had been in the line for days, was expected to play only a secondary role in the attack. The problem was the Côte Dame Marie, a crescent-shaped hill three hundred feet high and a kilometer long. The Germans used it as an observation place from which to call in artillery fire from batteries on the whaleback, the spine of hills that reached north from the AEF jump-off line, allowing them to control the central portion of the Meuse-Argonne. General Haan had sent his men forward against Dame Marie on October 13 in an attack that seemed successful. He sent a message to the Fifth Corps announcing its capture, which the Fifth Corps sent on to the First Army, Pershing's headquarters at the front. Haan believed that the general attack of October 14 was ordered because of his message. He felt that the only way he and his division could retain their reputation was to take the hill on October 14.

The plan of the First Army was that the Thirty-second would make a feint against the center of the hill while on the left the Forty-second Division (by that time in line in Fifth Corps) and on the right the Fifth Division (in Third Corps) would envelop the hill in a pincers and move north toward the heights of Barricourt. The heights marked the end of the rugged terrain that the AEF had been encountering. From there, the Meuse-Argonne sector leveled off into gently sloping terrain that stretched north and east to the Meuse. In the event, the pincers attack of October 14 failed, and the Thirty-second in its self-ordered attack took Côte Dame Marie. In a daring climb of the hill's east tip, Captain Edward B. Strom and seven men got within one hundred and fifty yards of the German defenders and forced their surrender by firing rifle grenades, all without an American casualty, killed or wounded.

2. Romagne was a part of the German line, but the local strong point was the Côte Dame Marie.

11. Romagne

1. Casualties in the Meuse-Argonne were 26,277 killed, 95,786 wounded

2. Baker excluded the Argonne Forest to the west of the Aire valley, the sector of the Seventy-seventh Division in First Corps.

3. Baker's narrative, unlike that of many enlisted men, shows no animus toward officers, and one must assume that here it was simply rank that concerned him.

4. The German Army used a crude flamethrowing mechanism, a tank carried by one soldier attached to a long hose carried by another, and the smoke might have been caused by flamethrowers. It seems unlikely, however, given the fact that the Germans were gradually withdrawing.

12. Relief

1. A red arrow on a shoulder patch designated the Thirty-second Division.

2. Camp Mills on Long Island was for troops waiting to embark from Hoboken for British or French ports and for returning soldiers after disembarking.

3. General Pershing in mid-October gave up command of the First Army, retaining his position as AEF commander. He divided the troops in the Meuse-Argonne by establishing Second Army, with First and Second under two newly promoted major generals, Lieutenant General Hunter Liggett, formerly commander of First Corps, and Lieutenant General Robert L. Bullard, from Third Corps. The bulk of the troops was in the First Army under Liggett, who immediately declared a virtual end to division attacks and took the last two weeks of October to rest the men. Rest included showers and boiling of clothes to kill the lice carried by almost all troops in the front line. Men received hot food brought up by rolling kitchens. Some went to hospitals, ill from pneumonia and diphtheria and, for a few, the influenza brought over from the United States by newly arriving troops (the German Army already was suffering from the worldwide pandemic of the autumn of 1918, as was the British Army). During all of the resting up, Liggett and corps and division commanders were preparing for the fourth attack in the Meuse-Argonne, November 1.

4. Jake was slang for "good." The commanding general of the Thirty-second, Haan, asked for the division's relief on October 17, as his units from brigades on down were much depleted. The new Fifth Corps commander, Charles P. Summerall, relieved the Thirty-second on October 20, grateful for its work in the line.

5. The Eighty-ninth would see a good deal of action. For ten days it occupied the northern edge of the Bois de Bantheville while the opposing Germans sent in patrols and otherwise drenched the area with mustard gas. After this purgatory and together with the Second Division on the left, which came up just before the attack of November 1, the Eighty-ninth had the task in the attack of advancing on the first day of the attack to the heights of Barricourt, thereafter to the Meuse and into the heights to the east of the river and with other divisions capturing the locations of the German batteries in the hills and advancing into the Woevre Plain.

6. Baker's pack had weighed the standard eighty pounds, but he left it at Romagne, where it was rifled, hence the lightness.

7. Casualties were 5,833, including 1,179 dead.

13. Cheppywald

1. A P.C. was a command post.

2. The Methodist church was split between northern and southern branches, a division caused by the slavery issue before the Civil War.

3. Baker's lack of lice may have been a result of cold weather and sleeping outside. Lice were carried by the rats that infested front and rear areas of the Meuse-Argonne. A German gassing of the Forty-second Division when in another sector resulted in extraordinary numbers of dead rats.

4. During attacks the members of the band acted as stretcher bearers, which also may not have appealed to Baker.

14. The Last Drive

1. The First was not going to the front but into reserve for Fifth Corps. In subsequent fighting it played a minor part.

2. At 6:00 a.m. on Armistice Day, November 11, General Pershing received word that the war would end at 11:00 in an armistice requested by delegates from the government in Berlin. His decision to continue fighting until the very end, with front-line units attacking, resulted in an uproar in Congress and a congressional investigation.

3. Several charitable organizations sponsored representatives in the AEF, some of whom were close to the front: the Red Cross, YMCA, Salvation Army, and Knights of Columbus.

4. The Rainbow or Forty-second Division had attempted the pincers above the Côte Dame Marie in company with the Fifth Division. Both failed in that effort, although the Eighty-fourth Brigade of the Forty-second captured the Côte de Chatillon, a part of the Kriemhilde Stellung, the German main line.

5. When General Liggett took First Army north on November 1–2 (First Corps moved toward Sedan beginning November 2), Fifth Corps captured the Barricourt heights, reached the great bend of the Meuse toward Mézières and Sedan, and together with Third Corps turned right, crossing the Meuse above Verdun. The 128th Infantry was crossing in this area. The Meuse was accompanied by a large canal. As Baker related, crossing it required two pontoon bridges, the canal needing a wide bridge because of flooding.

6. The Fifth Division began crossing the Meuse on November 3.

7. In the attempted pincer above Côte Dame Marie the commander of the Fifth Division, Major General John E. McMahon, proved unable to control his division and was replaced by a driving officer, Major General Hanson E. Ely, who turned the division around, evident in the Fifth's exploits to the east of the Meuse.

8. In the battle of the Masurian Lakes (1914), the Germans drove Russian forces into the lake country and captured 125,000.

15. Brandeville

1. The one-pounder was a 37-mm gun usually carried in a cart.

16. Alone in No-man's-land

1. The Woevre Plain east of the Meuse was the entrance to the German fortress of Metz, the goal of the newly established Second Army under General Bullard. Baker did not know that Second Army was planning an attack on Metz to begin November 14.

17. Ecurey

1. A Cossack post was a four-man outguard posting a single sentinel.

18. Peuvillers

1. The AEF in the person of General Pershing exhorted division commanders to use "accompanying guns" in front-line actions. The problem was twofold: the guns, 75s, could not get through forests or other rugged terrain; and, because of their weight, four tons, they required six-horse teams and drivers, which called attention to their presence. The chief of staff of First Army artillery, Colonel Conrad H. Lanza, studied the issue after the war and found that in sixty-two attempts with accompanying guns only three succeeded, all on November 1 or thereafter.

2. Whiz-bangs were Austrian 88s with shells that traveled faster than sound, so men in front of them did not hear the shells until after the explosions.

19. Armistice Day

1. Baker's exuberance was exaggerated; whole armies had surrendered before.

Bibliography

ARCHIVES

Library of Congress, Washington, D.C.
Frank Ross McCoy papers
National Archives, College Park, Md.
Thirty-second Division historical, 31 boxes, entry 1241, Record
    Group 120
U.S. Army Military History Institute, Carlisle Barracks, Carlisle, Pa.
Thirty-second Division survey, 11 boxes
Hale Hunt diary
Kenneth Gearhart Baker papers

BOOKS, ARTICLES, THESES

American Armies and Battlefields in Europe. Washington, D.C.: Gov-
    ernment Printing Office, 1938.
Bacevich, A. J. *Diplomat in Khaki: Major General Frank Ross McCoy
    and American Foreign Policy, 1898–1949*. Lawrence: University
    Press of Kansas, 1989.
Baker, Kenneth Gearhart. Edited by Robert H. Ferrell. "Oatmeal
    and Coffee." *Indiana Magazine of History* 97 (2001): 26–76.
Barry, John W. "The Midwest Goes to War: The 32nd Division in
    the Great War." Master's thesis, Towson State University,
    2005.
Braim, Paul F. *The Test of Battle: The American Expeditionary Forces in
    the Meuse-Argonne Campaign*. Newark: University of Delaware
    Press, 1987.

Cochrane, Rexmond C. *The Use of Gas in the Meuse-Argonne Campaign: September-November 1918.* Washington, D.C.: U.S. Army Chemical Corps, 1958.

Coffman, Edward M. *The Regulars: The Army Officer, 1898–1941.* Cambridge: Harvard University Press, 2004.

———. *The War to End All Wars: The American Military Experience in World War I.* New York: Oxford University Press, 1968.

DeWeerd, Harvey A. *President Wilson Fights His War: World War I and the American Intervention.* New York: Macmillan, 1968.

Eisenhower, John S. D. *Yanks: The Epic Story of the American Army in World War I.* New York: Free Press, 2001.

Ferrell, Robert H. *America's Deadliest Battle: Meuse-Argonne, 1918.* Lawrence: University Press of Kansas, 2007.

Fleming, Thomas J. *The Illusion of Victory: America in World War I.* New York: Basic Books, 2003.

Gansser, Emil B. *History of the 126th Infantry in the War with Germany.* Grand Rapids, Mich.: 126th Infantry Association, 1920.

Garlock, G. W. *Tales of the Thirty-Second.* West Salem, Wisc.: Badger, 1927.

Haan, William G. "The Division as a Fighting Machine." *Wisconsin Magazine of History* 4 (1920): 3–26.

Hamilton, Charles Granville. "Horace L. Baker, Educator and Historian." *Journal of Monroe County History* 5 (1979): 21–28.

Harbord, James G. *The American Army in France: 1917–1919.* Boston: Little, Brown, 1936.

Harries, Meiron, and Susie Harries. *The Last Days of Innocence: America at War, 1917–1918.* New York: Random House, 1997.

Jacobsmeyer, Paul J. "Intelligence in the American Expeditionary Force: The Experiences of the Thirty-second Division, September 1917-November 1918." Master's thesis, University of Wisconsin, 1986.

Millett, Allan R., and Williamson Murray, eds. *Military Effectiveness: The First World War.* Boston: Allen and Unwin, 1988.

Palmer, Frederick. *Our Greatest Battle (the Meuse-Argonne).* New York: Dodd, Mead, 1919.

Pershing, John J. *My Experiences in the World War.* 2 vols. New York: Stokes, 1931.

Persico, Joseph E. *Eleventh Month, Eleventh Day, Eleventh Hour: Armistice Day, 1918, World War I and its Violent Climax*. New York: Random House, 2004.

Prince, LaVerne. "Horace L. Baker." In *A History of Monroe County, Mississippi*. Dallas: Curtis, 1988.

Smythe, Donald. *Pershing: General of the Armies*. Bloomington: Indiana University Press, 1988.

The 32nd Division in the World War: 1917–1919. Milwaukee: Joint War Commission of Michigan and Wisconsin, 1920.

Thomas, Shipley. *The History of the A.E.F.* New York: Doran, 1920.

Vandiver, Frank E. *Black Jack: The Life and Times of John J. Pershing*. 2 vols. Fort Worth: Texas Christian University Press, 1977.

Van Every, Dale. *The A.E.F. in Battle*. New York: Appleton, 1928.

Venzon, Anne Cipriano, ed. *The United States in the First World War: An Encyclopedia*. New York: Garland, 1995.

Votaw, John F. *The American Expeditionary Forces in World War I*. Oxford, Eng.: Osprey, 2005.

Weigley, Russell F. *The American Way of War: A History of United States Military Strategy and Policy*. New York: Macmillan, 1971.

———. *History of the United States Army*. New York: Macmillan, 1967.

Index